CW01654642

prime®

The journey to **Supply Chain Excellence**

Buy

Deliver

Make

Demand

Plan

Foundation

Crimson&Co

With a foreword by Professor Jan Godsell, WMG, University of Warwick **Fourth edition**

Acknowledgements

This book is the result of a joint effort by the Crimson & Co team and thanks go to all of those involved in developing the material. Their dedication, knowledge and attitude remain a constant inspiration.

The content has been developed and honed over many client engagements, but particular appreciation is reserved for British American Tobacco (BAT). Through partnering with BAT, our research and experience has been tested, refined and repeatedly proven in a geographically diverse and complex supply chain. Special thanks go to Paul Reilly, Sean Mallon, Leonel Bolaños and Shaun Murkett and we would also like to acknowledge Phil Harris, Nicolas Wallimann and Tony Claringbould from the Global Manufacturing team who helped develop the Make profiles.

We would also like to thank Jan Godsell for a foreword which captures the essence of sc**prime**®.

Foreword

The supply chain is a key enabler of competitive advantage. Companies that have outperformed their rivals have supply chains that support their business strategy more effectively. This provides speed to market for new products, the ability to serve different channels efficiently, and the capability to adapt as business needs change or diversify.

Supply chain professionals ask similar questions: How mature are our current supply chain processes? How can they be improved? Do our people have the right capabilities? Where should we target the improvements for maximum benefit?

The profiles in this book are part of a toolkit developed to answer these questions. Supply chains are context specific, and the toolkit is structured so that the best practices within these pages can be customised to a particular business. This allows quite different organisations to develop strong, mature and ultimately 'excellent' processes and people capabilities across their supply chains.

The principles behind sc**prime**® are simple; generating step-change improvement in a supply chain to support business strategy. This book is a starting point on that journey.

Professor Jan Godsell, Operations and Supply Chain Strategy
WMG, University of Warwick

Foreword

The supply chain is a key enabler of competitive advantage. Companies that have outperformed their rivals have supply chains that support their business strategy more effectively. This provides speed to market for new products, the ability to serve different channels efficiently, and the capability to adapt as business needs change or diversify.

Supply chain professionals ask similar questions: How mature are our current supply chain processes? How can they be improved? Do our people have the right capabilities? Where should we target the improvements for maximum benefit?

The profiles in this book are part of a toolkit developed to answer these questions. Supply chains are context specific, and the toolkit is structured so that the best practices within these pages can be customised to a particular business. This allows quite different organisations to develop strong, mature and ultimately 'excellent' processes and people capabilities across their supply chains.

The principles behind sc**prime**® are simple; generating step-change improvement in a supply chain to support business strategy. This book is a starting point on that journey.

Professor Jan Godsell, Operations and Supply Chain Strategy
WMG, University of Warwick

Contents

Preface

sc**prime**® is Crimson & Co's powerful supply chain improvement approach, combining process and people capabilities for the first time so that the right people are in the right jobs, consistently doing the right things.

It is the result of many years of practical experience, identifying supply chain excellence in terms that are meaningful to each specific organisation and implementing in a way that generates sustainable improvement.

Using sc**prime**®, even the most complex business can be managed profitably whilst remaining innovative and adaptable, and rapid growth can be grasped whilst the business stays in control, minimising risk and making the most effective use of resources. sc**prime**® designs, trains and equips the supply chain so it meets the fast-changing needs of a business, continually seeking ways to generate extra competitive advantage.

The approach is well proven and has been used in over 20 countries on five continents. It identifies performance weaknesses and prioritises improvements; it prepares the ground for major IT implementations or acquisitions; and, it drives longer-term continuous improvement, becoming part of the culture and raising the standards of operations globally. In all instances, sc**prime**® is designed to ensure alignment of the supply chain with overall business strategy.

In contrast to other approaches, not only does sc**prime**® identify performance gaps and support target-setting, but it also shows how to close the gaps, directly translating actions into project plans so the business can quickly implement changes. Benefits are significant: operating costs are often reduced by 15%-20% and working capital by 10%-15%; responsiveness and service levels are improved and are more consistent, allowing greater innovation and driving increased sales; staff are developed according to the specific needs of the role, focusing on capabilities rather than job descriptions so they are equipped to carry out what is expected of them.

At the heart of sc**prime**® are best practice Excellence Profiles covering the full range of supply chain processes and a complete set of Capability Profiles, which identify what skills and experience are needed to complete the tasks. These are the focus of this book, but they are only part of the story;

sc**prime**® is an all-encompassing approach which includes vital techniques to ensure implementation is a success. Using these techniques, performance improvement and standardisation are inextricably aligned to the business as a whole; it is done by the business, not to the business, and becomes part of its core culture. That way lies sustainable success.

The supply chain keeps evolving and so does sc**prime**®. This is our fourth Edition, with substantial updated and additional content in areas such as procurement strategy, stakeholder management, supplier negotiations, cell strategy within production, spares management, and fleet maintenance & asset management. Notably, there are large additions in the form of contingency management and new product development, both areas which have seen increased emphasis in recent years. The update also includes case studies of blue-chip organisations that have successfully improved elements of their supply chain processes following an sc**prime**® assessment, including a leading global pharmaceutical company and a global wine company.

Since the previous edition we have also launched a new online sc**prime**® tool. This allows supply chain leaders to perform a self-assessment online and receive an instant report which benchmarks their processes against industry best practice and identifies improvement opportunities.

The journey to supply chain excellence continues!

Introduction

sc**prime**® uses the latest best practice benchmarks, detailed process descriptions and in-depth people capability profiles to offer businesses a unique way to see how good they are, understand what they need to do to improve, and develop a team that will get them there. It aligns people and processes to ensure that a business can create and maintain competitive advantage through its supply chain.

This book describes the sc**prime**® approach, but it is worth considering how it can be used and what questions it can help answer, because this is where its power becomes clear.

The Board agenda

For senior executives, the supply chain is usually only one of many functional areas competing for their attention, and of key importance are more general issues such as: managing growth or decline; the balance sheet, especially cash; the P&L; share price/company value; consistency of performance; continued track record of success; and, controlling and limiting risk.

These issues can be phrased in many different ways, but the consistent theme is that the specifics of the supply chain operation are not always foremost in mind.

- What should we focus on as a business?
- How do we know that we are doing the right things?
- How do we build a business that is quick enough to respond to market changes?
- Do we have the right people with the right capabilities and do they understand what to do?
- How do we deal with complexity without simplifying away all the value?
- How do we actually get our people to ‘do’ the strategy?

sc**prime**® can be used to answer all these questions, and more, and so helps senior executives to address their most prominent challenges;

- Detailed process descriptions describe what the business should do to deliver its strategy, and the benchmarks show which areas need special focus. The workforce is developed and empowered so that it has the capability and motivation to carry out what is needed, using a mechanism that allows total transparency at each management level

- Improvement actions are developed into formal projects with individual business cases showing the impact on profit, cash and service, driving real benefit to customers and the bottom line

- Robust yet adaptable processes can be designed and standardised for dealing with high levels of innovation and market change, allowing shorter time-to-market, more frequent product innovation and the ability to enter and exit markets in a controlled way

- Diversity can be built-in, and yet processes harmonised across the business, allowing complexity and creativity to co-exist with control, clarity and consistency

- Ongoing measurement and monitoring processes, coupled with empowered workforces in local business units, ensure that changes are sustained

- Diagnostic tools and ongoing change controls minimise business risk and maximise financial return for major initiatives such as large-scale IT implementations and M&A integrations. Any potential challenges are identified well in advance and, throughout, the fundamental issues of processes and people are addressed

- Key appointments, and subsequent training and development, are more successful as they are based on the precise capabilities needed to carry out the role in a particular business with its own, specific ways of working

The supply chain professional's needs

Senior supply chain managers are involved in strategic discussions and are faced with some or all of the issues above. At different levels of management and operation, they also become more heavily involved in the detail as they are inevitably tasked with making it work in practice.

sc**prime**® has been designed to be used by staff at all levels within the supply chain and to provide practical guidance and insight when seeking to develop supply chain processes or to identify and improve people capabilities.

One of the strengths of sc**prime**® is that it is fact-driven and detailed. It shows for each level of excellence what a business actually has to do, at an activity level. It is completely objective and allows unequivocal gaps to be identified between current and expected performance. This clarity and understanding at a detailed level brings many benefits:

- The process definitions can be used across multiple sites and multiple businesses to create a common language for discussion and understanding. This is especially useful when it is important to work closely with outsourced or other third party operations, and can be a driver for joint improvement programmes and more effective collaboration

- The change management challenge is lessened by the clear presentation of fact at a level that is both understandable and usable by operators

- The outputs can be picked up by an operator and the actions they need to take are clear: the process capability outputs show what the business has to do in any specific area to move from what it is doing now to what it wants to be doing in the future. The people capability outputs similarly show what a person in a particular role in a particular business needs to be able to do

Supply chain professionals are frequently tasked with designing continuous improvement programmes. sc**prime**® takes this to the next level; it empowers operators to generate repeated step-change whilst knowing they are totally aligned with business strategy.

Improvements

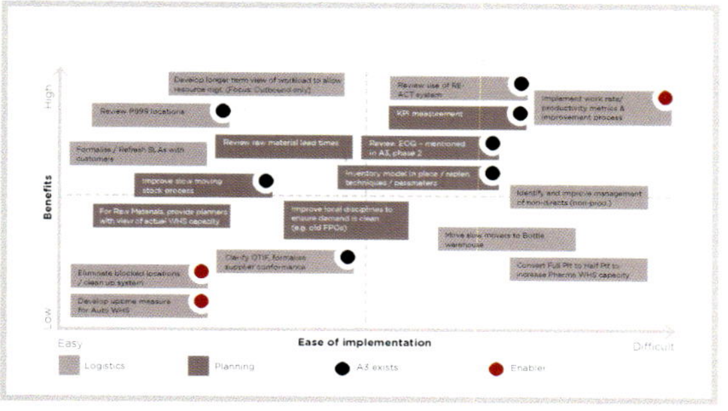

Benefits

Opportunities to reduce inventory by over €100m and annual operating costs by €2m were identified across EMEA sites. A programme to deliver these savings was developed, phased over 12-18 months. This was based on regional best practice sharing and establishing a logistics best practice community in the region. The client was left with a toolkit to enable ongoing continuous improvement.

Savings targets

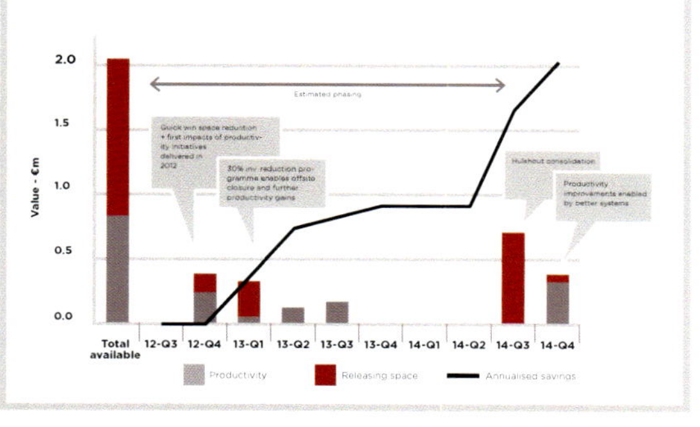

Case study: Systems implementation (dairy foods company)

Background

Our client was implementing an advanced planning system as part of a wider Integrated Business Planning project to improve performance across its operating divisions. The decision was taken to use a phased introduction of system modules together with a new Sales and Operations Planning (S&OP) process:

Phase 1: Demand forecasting and activity management workflow
Phase 2: Supply planning and network optimisation
Phase 3: Site schedule optimisation

Application

sc**prime**® was used to define the expected process maturity by phase, assuming the introduction of related system functionality. This allowed a detailed process improvement road map to be developed alongside system requirements.

Phased maturity roadmap

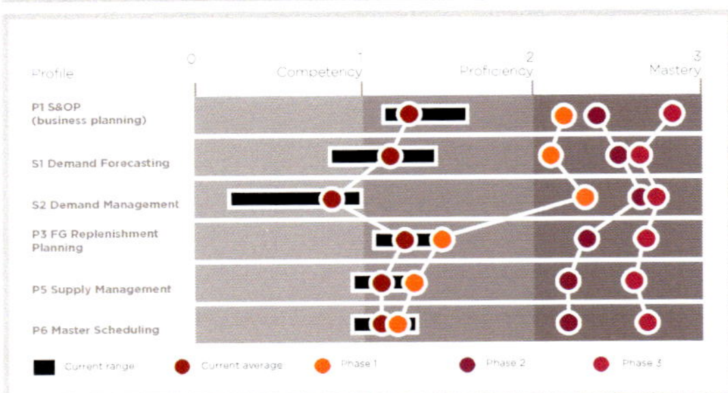

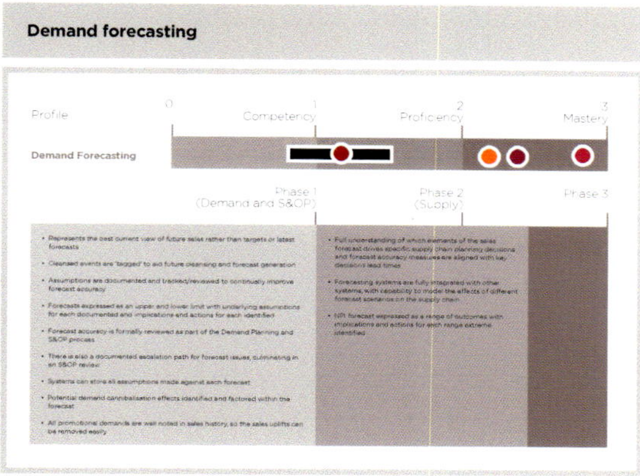

Benefits

The to-be business processes provided clarity and understanding to the relevant stakeholders, including how they would deliver tangible performance improvements. System functionality was driven by process requirements rather than being systems-led, which meant that unnecessary system module configuration costs and licensing fees were avoided.

Case study: Procurement transformation diagnostic (major airports group)

Background

Our client, historically a public sector organisation, now had new private equity investors and executive leadership and was embarking on a major transformation to 'world class' in preparation for an acquisition programme. Based locally on four operating sites, its procurement functions were poorly aligned and had limited presence in the business. The client wanted to improve and standardise Procurement effectiveness across its operations with the aims of increasing procurement alignment to the business, significant cost reduction and increased capability.

Application

scprime® was used to establish the as-is, define the to-be and identify the activities to bridge the gaps. Working with key stakeholders in the business, it gave a clear and unambiguous framework to assess the disparate operations. These inputs were used in a series of workshops to develop a detailed improvement roadmap and implementation plan.

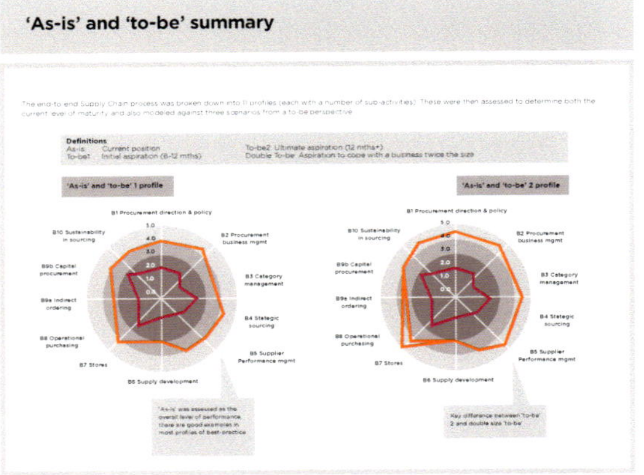

Procurement profiles reviewed

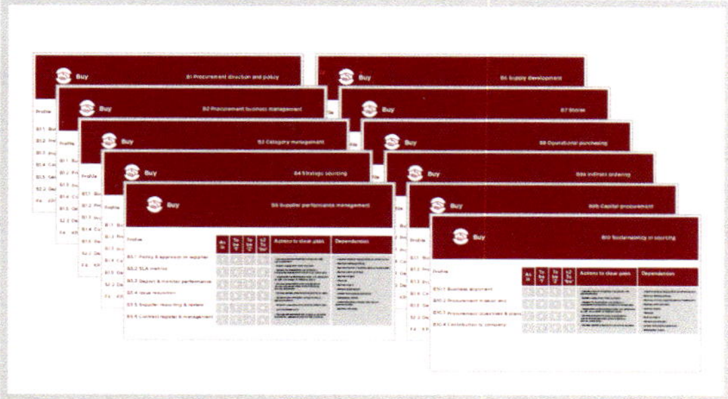

Implementation road map

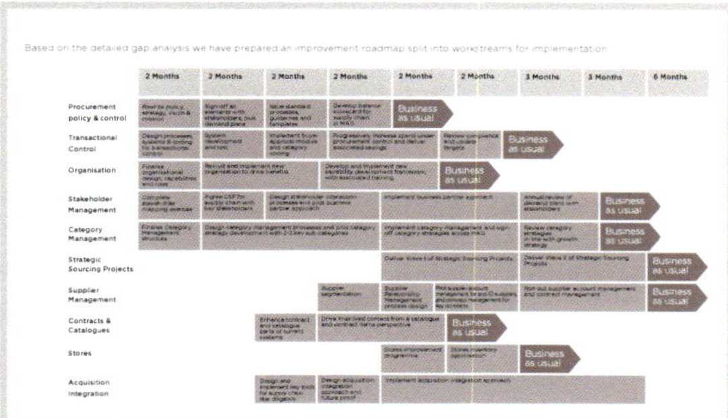

Benefits

The improvement roadmap targeted procurement savings of 15% over a five year period. This savings delivery programme was supported by nine workstreams and a new organisation structure. There was excellent support from key stakeholders across the business through their involvement in the sc**prime**® based diagnostic. The implementation plan was then integrated into the wider business improvement and implementation programme.

Case study: People capabilities (global wine company)

Background

Our client was beginning to implement a global planning hub and wanted to ensure that the project focused equally on systems, processes and people. The business was unsure if the existing teams could handle the new global ways of working and wanted to understand where risks might be, to tackle them proactively.

Application

The future operating model was translated into new operating processes and a new organisational design. Role profiles were created and sc**prime**® was used to identify the capabilities that would be required to operate the future processes to the desired operational standards.

120 people around the world completed the sc**prime**® self-assessment survey, rating their own knowledge and understanding. The scores were moderated by the management team and then analysed against the target levels at a job, department and individual level. This provided an objective overall view of the gaps between current and target capability levels. An action plan was drawn up to close the capability gaps through either classroom training sessions, on the job development or redeployment and recruitment.

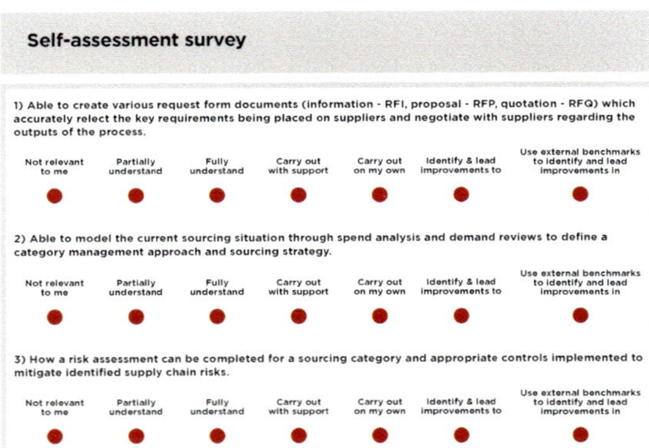

Self-assessment survey

1) Able to create various request form documents (information - RFI, proposal - RFP, quotation - RFQ) which accurately relect the key requirements being placed on suppliers and negotiate with suppliers regarding the outputs of the process.

Not relevant to me	Partially understand	Fully understand	Carry out with support	Carry out on my own	Identify & lead improvements to	Use external benchmarks to identify and lead improvements in

2) Able to model the current sourcing situation through spend analysis and demand reviews to define a category management approach and sourcing strategy.

Not relevant to me	Partially understand	Fully understand	Carry out with support	Carry out on my own	Identify & lead improvements to	Use external benchmarks to identify and lead improvements in

3) How a risk assessment can be completed for a sourcing category and appropriate controls implemented to mitigate identified supply chain risks.

Not relevant to me	Partially understand	Fully understand	Carry out with support	Carry out on my own	Identify & lead improvements to	Use external benchmarks to identify and lead improvements in

Gap analysis

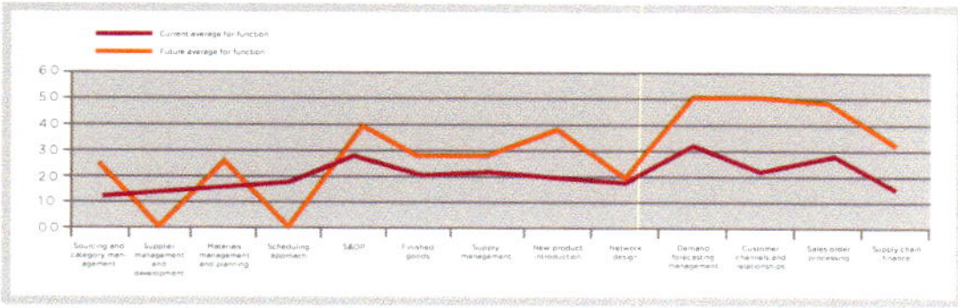

Benefits

The use of the sc**prime**® people capabilities tool greatly simplified the process of assessing this global population of supply chain professionals. Skills enhancements were then focused on specific capability gaps, meaning that more cost effective solutions could be deployed, and the capability-based role profiles supported both HR in their recruitment tasks and line managers in their staff development planning. The overall capability development programme ensured that the business maximised the impact of its systems investment.

New innovative online self-assessment tool

Our new online self-assessment tool is part of the powerful sc**prime**® improvement approach. Use sc**prime**® online to perform a self-assessment on up to three profiles and receive an instant detailed report which benchmarks your processes against industry best practice and identifies improvement opportunities. For your own self-assessment, visit www.crimsonandco.com, go to the sc**prime**® webpage and simply register to start.

1. Choose a profile

Once registered, you will then be able to carry out a self-assessment on up to three profiles. Click a profile to find out more and then click 'Start' if you would like to self-assess on this chosen profile. Alternatively click 'Back' to find out more about another profile. Once you click 'Start' one of your three complimentary profiles will be used.

2. Self-assess

The self-assessment should take no more than 10 minutes to complete and is made up of a series of statements, which you answer true or false. Please answer with the response that is best aligned to your processes. For the purposes of the self-assessment, if a statement is not applicable, simply answer 'True'. The progress bar towards the top of the screen will indicate how far through the self-assessment you are and you can stop at any time as the system will auto-save your answers.

3. Report

On clicking 'submit', a detailed report will instantly be emailed to you. You can also view your report by clicking the 'view' button, which will open the report as a pdf file in a separate window. The report contains an overall maturity score for the assessed profile, along with detail on how well you meet the 'Competency', 'Proficiency' and 'Mastery' criteria, as well as identifying the most relevant changes needed to improve the processes.

This online self-assessment tool has been designed to give a taste of what sc**prime**® can offer. We normally work collaboratively with clients to explore current levels of maturity and future improvement opportunities in detail through interviews, process mapping and structured workshops. If you would like to understand more about the improvement opportunities contained in the emailed report and the others that may be open to you, please contact us and we will set up a face-to-face session to explore them. We would also be delighted to get feedback on how easy you found our sc**prime**® online tool to use and how useful you found it.

"The sc**prime**® online tool is easy to use, easy to understand and the reporting is quick. The site will enable our Global Operations to assess our supply chain business process capability with an efficient and consistent approach."
John Burdett,
VP Global Operations Planning, Tata Global Beverages

1 - Choose a profile

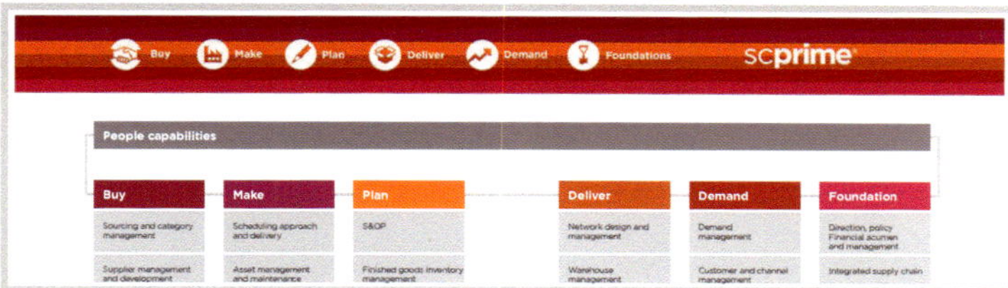

2 - Self-assess

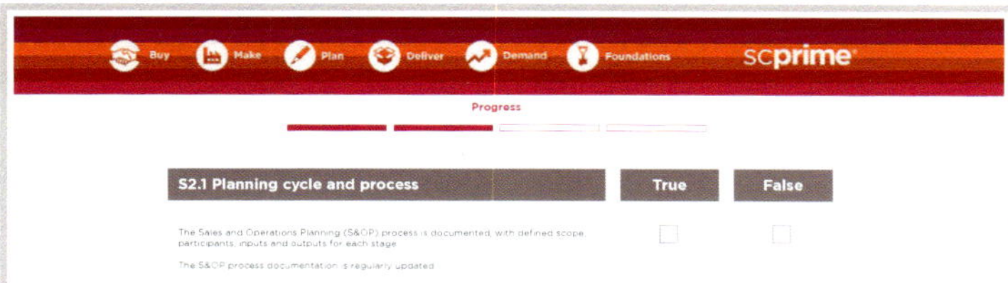

3 - Receive your report

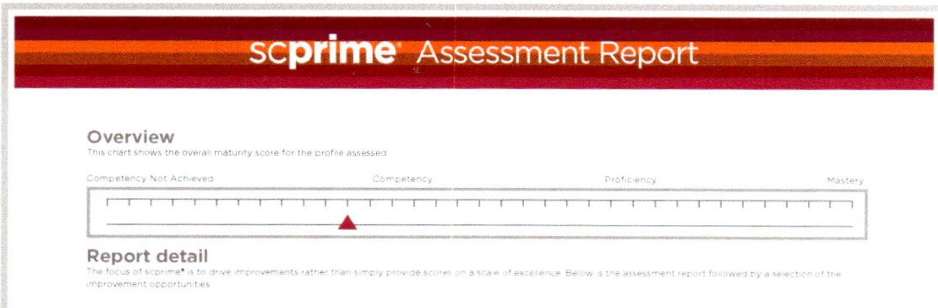

Process capabilities

Introduction

sc**prime**® uses a different sort of benchmarking approach based on business processes. Applicable to a wide range of businesses, it is designed to drive action; business units can clearly see how they can get better across their whole range of business processes. It is also focused on a company's strategic objectives; it turns strategy into reality. This can be through process improvement and/or standardisation, cost reduction or simply identifying and fixing weaknesses in the supply chain. In all cases, it can be customised to address the specific business needs.

Benchmarking is widespread but it is often misused. The most common example of this relates to 'quantitative' benchmarking, which focuses on metrics, usually comparing costs, working capital or service levels against those of other companies. This is sometimes facilitated by 'benchmarking clubs' and can be an interesting angle, and a prompt to re-examine some supply chain fundamentals.

However, quantitative benchmarking has two major drawbacks. First, differences in metrics can simply be due to differences in business models, products or customer characteristics. For example, a business using distributors as a route to market will have lower finished goods inventories than another which controls the supply chain to final customer delivery; and, small, light products have lower distribution costs compared to bulky products. Second, the technique says little about how to improve. How do you close the gap in performance?

So, although benefits of this approach do exist, quantitative benchmarking must be approached with care; it is not a complete solution.

'Process' benchmarking, in contrast, tends to have a deeper impact since robust, effective processes are the building blocks of a profitable and competitive organisation. Measuring process excellence against a standard can give an accurate view of capability in each part of a business, although the first challenge is always to select the right standard, recognising that the most appropriate comparison source might differ for each business area.

The essential element in selecting the standards, or targets, is understanding what drives competitive advantage for the business. At what does a business merely have to do 'well' and at what must it excel? Just doing 'well' might mean targeting best practice in that sector, but for the areas where competitive advantage is sought, a wider sector view is needed. The key is to focus on what the business wants to achieve.

Having undertaken process benchmarking consistently over the past twenty years, across a multitude of sectors including consumer goods, retail, pharmaceuticals, beverages, aerospace, telecoms, automotive, industrial and utilities, it is clear that some critical elements are required to create real, lasting and useful improvements: there must be a close fit with a company's specific business objectives and needs; there must be a focus on the improvement path; and, the business must believe the benchmarks and 'own' the results.

sc**prime**® is based on these principles. It has supply chain-wide process benchmarks which are modular and can be customised. They are also in roadmap format, showing the path to excellence. It also has other elements, part of the overall 'toolkit', which can be packaged into a complete solution to drive improvement in the short, medium and long term.

This approach has been thoroughly proven with multinational businesses, having been customised to their specific needs. The results are both effective and long-lasting, as well as being hard-linked to company strategy and objectives. sc**prime**® turns strategy into reality and drives sustainable growth.

1 What is the scprime® process capability framework?

The sc**prime**® process capability framework is based on a set of process definitions which give a comprehensive view of best practice across the supply chain, enabling benchmarking to take place and improvements to be generated.

The structure is modular so that it can be easily applied to different entities. There are a number of Excellence Profiles within each functional area and a particular organisation or business unit can assemble the appropriate profiles to reflect its own functions.

The profiles are split into elements, each describing aspects of a process at various levels of excellence (see the diagram on the next page). The elements are fact-based, not subjective, and they allow easy and unambiguous scoring.

The process definitions are at a detailed level and reflect regularly-updated best practice based on real experience. They allow a thorough and objective assessment of strengths and weaknesses across operations, regionally or globally.

Roadmap to best practice

- Definition of relevant best practice, and stages of maturity
- Customised to the industry and company strategy
- Roadmaps evolve with business needs

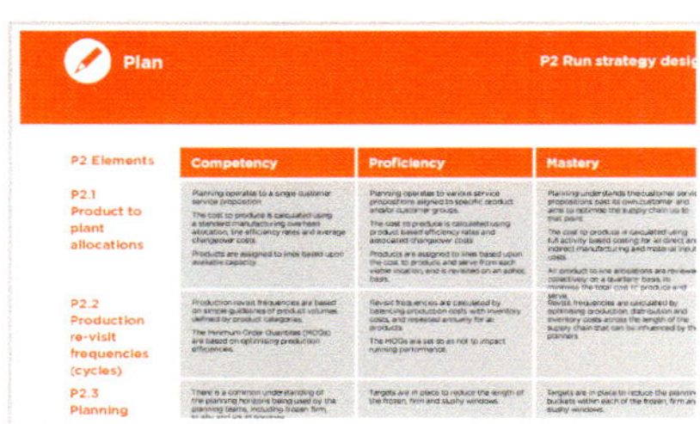

Supply chain excellence

Buy	Make	Plan
Procurement direction & policy	Production strategy	S&OP
Procurement business management	Detailed scheduling	Run strategy design
Category management	Asset maintenance	Finished goods inventory management
Strategic sourcing	Production systems	Finished goods replenishment planning
Supplier performance management	High performing teams	Strategic supply planning
Supply development	Sustainability in manufacturing	Tactical supply planning
Operational purchasing		Materials inventory management
Indirect procurement		Materials replenishment management
Capital procurement		New product introduction
Sustainability in sourcing		Sustainability in planning

Deliver	Demand	Foundation
Network design & management	Demand forecasting	Integrated working
Warehouse planning	Demand management	Education and training
Warehouse operations	Customer relationship management	Data management and integrity
Warehouse performance management	Sales order processing	KPI reporting
Transport operations	Customer & channel segmentation	Continual improvement
Transport performance management	New product development	Quality assurance
Contractor management	Promotion planning	Contingency management
Sustainability in delivery	Sustainability in demand	Sustainability strategy

Other parts of the sc**prime**® framework support the use of the best practice profiles, for example:

- 'How-To' guides are a set of standard methods of moving a site up the process excellence scale. They define how to address weaknesses in specific functional areas. For example, a How-To guide for Materials Planning will define the standard materials planning processes to be followed, system parameters and screens, and roles and responsibilities, amongst others. It will also define how to make the changes as part of a focused project

- An sc**prime**® intranet site is a useful facility to enable best practice sharing and build a community around the improvement programme

- A training course for assessors is required to ensure high quality assessments. This should cover general questioning and assessment skills and techniques as well as the specific functional content.

Our approach

At the heart of sc**prime**® is an 'improvement cycle', where sites are assessed and their performance improved.

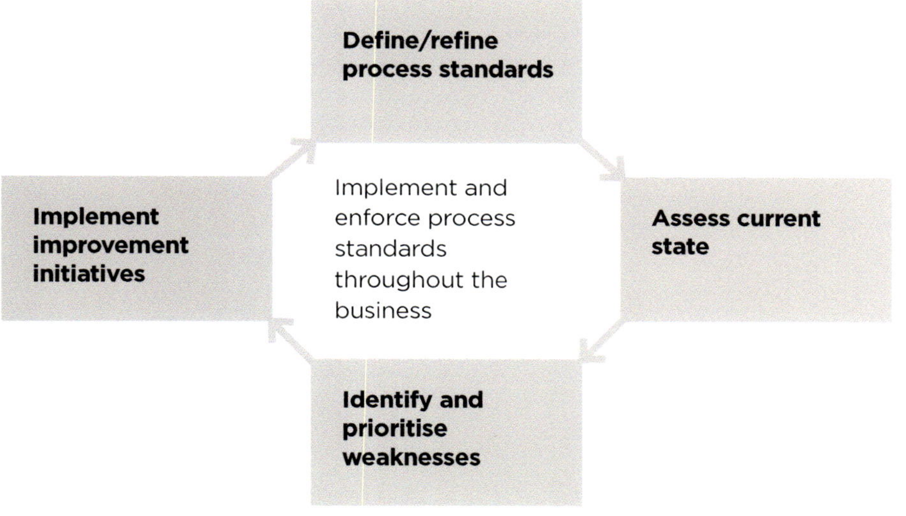

An assessment report shows scores per function, and per profile, against agreed company targets.

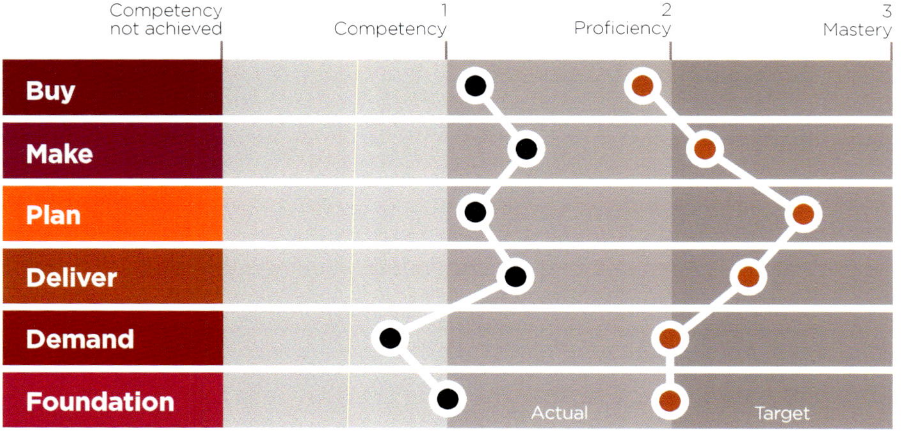

Based on these reports, action plans are developed in line with agreed strategic aims. The focus of sc**prime**® is to drive improvement rather than simply to provide scores on a scale of excellence.

sc**prime**® impacts a business in two stages:

- **Functional Improvement**
  Getting better at making, moving and buying, for example

- **Cross functional Improvement**
  Developing more effective planning and other business-wide processes

The potential supply chain benefits are considerable, especially in multinational businesses:

	Functional	Cross-Functional
Adminstration Overhead		Less crisis management, progress chasing **15% saving**
Freight	Load fill optimisation **30% saving**	
Warehousing/ inventory	3PL contract/productivity management **15% saving**	Stock reduction **50% finished goods reduction**
Factory overhead	Lean manufacturing **40% less waste**	Less crisis management, progress chasing **15% saving**
Factory direct	Reduced downtime **40% increase in productivity**	Less disruption, better run strategies **10% less waste**
Packaging	Best practice procurement procedures **2% price reduction**	VMI (where appropriate), flow optimisation **1% price reduction**
Ingredients	Effective supplier interaction **Price reductions**	Demand visibility **Price reductions**

This has a direct positive impact on a company's financial statements:

Functional area	Balance sheet	P&L
Buy	Lower working capital (raw materials) **30-40%**	Lower raw materials costs **3-5%** Lower indirect materials costs **5-10%**
Make	Higher return on capital employed (ROCE) **5-10%**	Lower manufacturing costs **10-15%**
Plan	Lower working capital (finished goods) **30-40%**	Lower supply chain costs **10-15%**
Deliver		Lower distribution costs **10-15%**
Demand		Increase in sales **3-5%**

Using sc**prime**®

sc**prime**® can be used in various ways to support different business needs:

- The Excellence Profiles can be used as they stand for a quick assessment of operations against cross-industry best practice. Rapid, one-off improvement actions can then be put in place

- Where specific problem areas are known, the appropriate profiles can be used to understand the causes of the problems and how to resolve them

- Where operations are being merged, or where two businesses want to assess synergies, the profiles can be used to identify differences between ways of working and the actions and effort required to standardise and raise both parties to the same level of performance

- For large systems implementations, the profiles can be used to understand how different parts of a business really operate before a uniform system is imposed, so that functionality can be clarified for the systems build and potential implementation problems can be identified well in advance

The power of sc**prime**® is maximised when it is built into the DNA of a business. This means customised solutions, aligned to company strategy or specific business needs, using the terminology of the business and run by people in the business.

This is most often seen in the development of business-wide, sustainable improvement programmes, which typically follow four main steps.

1. Tailor the solution

sc**prime**® is modular and can be customised; Excellence Profiles can be aligned with a specific industry and organisation, reflecting the business needs and terminology.

A decision also needs to be made on targets and follow-ups. Generally an organisation will set 'minimum' standards based on business risks; any site with process standards below this level will have to act quickly to improve.

There will also be 'expected' standards, required for an effective end-to-end supply chain. Finally, there are 'stretch' standards, desired for key/strategic sites. sc**prime**® also uses other tools, such as introductory documentation, score sheets and assessment feedback templates. Any implementation will generally require a small scale pilot for testing and fine-tuning purposes.

2. Design an assessment/improvement programme

The assessment programme should be designed to meet specific business needs. In most cases a schedule is developed to assess the more strategic sites more frequently, perhaps every eighteen months. Other sites can be assessed every two years.

The 'improvement cycle' needs to be designed to generate a set of improvement actions from each assessment. These actions will need monitoring, either by global or regional resources. Finally, the next assessment of that site in the programme will ensure that the improvements have been implemented and embedded.

3. Kick-off the assessment programme

The assessment programme will require appropriate resources to carry out assessments, to monitor improvement plans, and to manage and keep the toolkit updated.

Once resources are in place, the assessment programme can be kicked-off. A site assessment will take anything between three and ten days depending on scope. Outputs include process excellence scores, gaps and improvement plans. These are documented, agreed, and actioned. Improvement plans should be prioritised based on company-wide and local strategy.

4. Monitor and adjust

The sc**prime**® solution needs to be managed and kept up-to-date. All users should provide feedback on usability and usefulness of each part of the solution. In some cases immediate changes can be made. Other suggestions can be saved for a periodic review of the profile content and broader solution, carried out every twelve to eighteen months. This should also reflect changes to company strategy.

Buy

- Procurement direction & policy
- Procurement business management
- Category management
- Strategic sourcing
- Supplier performance management
- Supply development
- Operational purchasing
- Indirect procurement
- Capital procurement
- Sustainability in sourcing

2 Buy

Procurement and supply management are increasingly important as organisations face the challenge of improving the quality of products and services while decreasing costs. The value of bought in goods and services represents a significant proportion of an organisation's revenue (30% - 80%) so improvements in the Buy function can have a dramatic impact on an organisation's bottom line. Good management of the Buy function can also deliver other significant benefits including robust risk management, innovation and supply chain agility.

The Buy processes encompass the initial sourcing decision, the on-going relationship with suppliers and the smooth flow of goods and services from the supplier to the purchasing organisation. To operate effectively, the Buy processes should have documented strategies that are agreed with the wider business.

Supply chains start with buying goods and services; they are the 'inputs' to an organisation's production process. Problems in the Buy area can often manifest themselves further down the supply chain, so getting these processes right is of paramount importance if a supply chain is to operate efficiently and effectively. Indeed, the people involved in procurement decisions must work together to deliver the optimal solution for an organisation and this approach must be supported by the Board, consistent with the company's objectives and compatible with culture and structure.

The process begins with the definition of a company's sourcing strategy; what is required, and how the company wishes to work with its suppliers. A well defined strategy will ensure that a company has a firm operational basis from which to work, and a clear understanding of the costs it is likely to incur.

This overall strategy should be supported by detailed procurement category strategies that articulate how each category will be approached by the buying organisation. This should be executed by a robust strategic sourcing process to obtain the required goods and services at the most appropriate total cost.

Procurement and supply management can deliver benefits beyond cost reductions. Good relationships with suppliers allow existing products to be improved and new products to be rapidly brought to market. Security of supply and better risk control are often the result of supplier collaboration. In addition to this, process efficiency and continuous improvement can be delivered through good management of the Buy function.

This chapter outlines the different sections of the Buy function, and each element contained therein. By increasing maturity in relevant elements, an organisation can deliver the benefits outlined above. The topics include procurement direction and policy, procurement business management, category management, strategic sourcing, supplier performance management, supply development, operational purchasing, indirect procurement, capital procurement and sustainability in sourcing.

Procurement direction ensures the function has a clear mission, supported by goals and plans which are aligned to the wider business.

Description

This profile is applicable at the global, regional and local levels. The objective is to ensure that cyclical procurement planning produces clear missions, goals and clearly defined critical success factors. The outputs usually take the form of a procurement-specific mission statement, vision and objectives which cascade through to individual targets and are supported by relevant policies and procedures. The output is also used to ensure procurement aligns its objectives with those of the broader organisation, and to give transparency to procurement activity of other functions.

Context

Procurement direction and policy encompasses the effective leadership, control and steering of the function. When effective, it leads to clarity and alignment and supports the procurement function's effort to contribute directly to the performance of the business, within a clear policy. Lack of strength in this area, as well as the obvious impact of a lack of direction and vision in procurement, will generally lead to a silo approach, where procurement is insular and the broader business lacks awareness of the value of the function.

Glossary

CSF

Abbreviation for Critical Success Factors - those activities and processes that must be done to enable the company to reach its goals.

B1 Procurement direction and policy

B1 Elements	Competency	Proficiency	Mastery
B1.1 Business alignment	A procurement policy is in place which is used internally within procurement and is available to the business. Business needs have been identified when devising the policy. Updates are signed off within Procurement. The scope of the procurement policy is all external expenditure.	The procurement policy is aligned to global and regional requirements. Business needs have been identified and aligned on a global basis when devising the policy. Updates are made and communicated to the entire organisation. The policy is signed off at a business unit level. User satisfaction is reviewed.	The procurement policy has been comprehensively communicated and adopted within the organisation. There is a full understanding of the greater needs and goals of the overall business and their cascading consequences on procurement. The policy is reviewed and signed off at defined intervals. User compliance to policy is tracked and actioned. User satisfaction is reviewed proactively at agreed intervals.
B1.2 Procurement strategy	A distinct vision of procurement direction is in place. Key individuals within the function understand the procurement strategy.	A procurement-specific strategy and vision exists. The executive and senior teams have a detailed understanding of the procurement strategy. The understanding of the strategy within the function is consistent.	The procurement strategy is fully aligned with the strategic vision of the company. Full transparency is in place, with good understanding of the procurement strategy across the business and new communication following updates. Overall success is measured by the unprompted awareness and understanding of procurement vision and objectives within non-procurement functions.

B1 Elements	Competency	Proficiency	Mastery
B1.3 Procurement objective and plans	Procurement plans and objectives are in place and are formulated on an annual basis. Procurement plans are based on historical spend. Financial targets are agreed with Finance.	Procurement plans and financial targets are agreed by stakeholders. Financial targets are incorporated into broader company plans. Procurement plans also take account of demand forecasts. The plan is regularly reviewed within the procurement function and used to measure functional activities.	Comprehensive, well documented plans and objectives are developed with stakeholders and agreed by budget holders and Finance. Plans are aligned to and integrated with the company plan. Progress against the plan is regularly updated to stakeholders.
B1.4 Contribution to company performance	Performance requirements are agreed. The Critical Success Factors (CSFs) for Procurement are defined.	Performance is monitored. The senior team have visibility of procurement contribution. The CSFs are aligned with the mission of the overall organisation. Procurement KPIs are reported monthly.	Performance is monitored and audited as an integral part of continuous improvements. Active promotion of procurement contribution is evident through defined channels. The CSFs are systematically reviewed as a part of broader reviews. A procurement balanced scorecard which contributes to organisational performance is reported monthly.
B1.5 General procurement guidelines	General procurement guidelines are defined and used within Procurement. The organisation has an understanding of the need for and application of best practice procurement.	General procurement guidelines are shared and applied across the organisation. Procurement guidelines are consistent with the style and content of broader business guidelines.	Guidelines are consistent with other corporate material and reviewed regularly in conjunction with broader business material. There is consistent evidence of the application of procurement best practice across the organisation.

Procurement business management is the operation of the procurement function in delivering the mission and vision set out by direction and policy.

Description

This profile applies at the functional level. Where direction and policy set the vision and objectives of the procurement function within an organisation, this profile focuses on how that is delivered; how the procurement team works as a unit of the business, how those within it are managed and how their interface with the rest of the business is managed.

Context

Procurement business management is the foundation for delivery of the procurement vision and all the other value adding activities that occur. It considers the function as an organisation, stripping away the procurement objectives and mission to measure the effectiveness of the function as a business unit with employees, a clear purpose, and a position within the overall business. Effective management will deliver benefits similar to those of an effectively managed business, with low staff turnover, fairly rewarded team members with good morale and a good image in the broader business and with stakeholders. Poor performance in this area is often demonstrated by a lack of clarity, compliance and varying processes.

Buy

B2 Procurement business management

Procurement business management is the operation of the procurement function in delivering the mission and vision set out by direction and policy.

Glossary

SLAs

Abbreviation for a Service Level Agreement, an agreement between the supplying and receiving parties defining how the service is provided. At its most basic, an SLA details service and quality levels, but can cover every aspect of supply from cost, delivery, returns, innovation and improvement. The SLA usually forms a part of the contract between the two parties.

Buy

B2 Procurement business management

B2 Elements	Competency	Proficiency	Mastery
B2.1 People and organisation	A procurement group exists with clear reporting lines and accountability. High level resource plans exist. Job specifications exist.	Organisational responsibilities are in line with procurement strategy (e.g. category management, geography). The Procurement staff have relevant knowledge and expertise. The Procurement team and Human Resources work together in recruitment with selection criteria supported by clear job specifications. There is a defined induction process. The Procurement staff are actively managed through personal objectives.	The Procurement team structure is dictated by procurement policy. The Procurement staff have clear development plans and personal objectives aligned to performance requirements. Recruitment sits under a company-wide process, with roles advertised extensively with tailored specifications. There are comprehensive recruitment selection criteria including qualifications, experience and behavioural competencies. The induction processes includes an introduction to the Procurement function and the broader business.
B2.2 Clarity of purpose	Basic or core roles and responsibilities are defined. The Procurement function is recognised as owning external expenditure within the business. Strategic procurement is differentiated from transactional purchasing.	Roles and responsibilities are clearly defined within the Procurement function (e.g. commodity responsibility, negotiation, material control). Clearly defined job descriptions are in place. The Procurement staff are skilled/trained appropriately according to their role and/or grade. There is procurement representation in the business leadership team.	There is role flexibility permitting effective rotation of staff. Job descriptions are signed off by function head. The Procurement function is recognised as central to core activities, managing a high proportion of the total spend. The Procurement function has strong sponsorship from the Executive team.

B2 Elements	Competency	Proficiency	Mastery
B2.3 Performance management	Appropriate KPIs are in place to measure and report individual performance. There is a formal assessment of professional procurement skills. A reward system is in place.	A formal appraisal scheme with KPIs is in place. There is a formal assessment of soft skills, business and financial understanding. Development plans are driven by organisational needs. Professional certification is encouraged. Development plans and reward systems are linked to the appraisal process, with alignment to career planning and training.	Comprehensive appraisal methodologies are used to track and drive performance. There is a consistent company development process integrated with organisational planning. Professional accreditation needs are determined on an individual basis. Professional and personal development are actively supported. There is an integrated approach to individual and team recognition.
B2.4 Compliance	There is transaction monitoring for compliance to policy. The need for compliance is understood by the Procurement team.	Compliance targets and controls are set and tracked for all goods and services. There is a fully documented process for how requirements become purchases, which is consistently applied.	Compliance to procurement processes is part of the overall supply chain management process, with integrated measures across the organisation. There is a value based trade-off between compliance and process efficiency.

B2.5 Strategy for processes and enabling technologies	There is a structured approach for procurement processes and technology. Technology plans exist, supporting tactical business needs. Management reports exist.	Procurement processes are effective. There is a commonality of processes across functions, with processes well documented and good compliance and levels of staff understanding. Formal technology plans are defined and focused on efficiency. Key data is accessible with transactional reporting capability. There is good visibility of management reports in the Procurement function.	Procurement processes are regularly reviewed and improved to take account of latest developments. Procurement practices allow flexibility to suit local or specific variations. The technology plan is aligned to the procurement strategy. Technology plans are integrated with key supply partners. There is good visibility of management reporting, with suitable alerts, across the entire organisation. There is easy access to all data, with user-friendly management reports in place.
B2.6 Stakeholder management	There are business reviews with key stakeholders, with a focus on operational improvement. Key data is captured and regularly updated. Effective management of the business partnership between Procurement and relevant stakeholder groups exists.	There are annual strategic reviews with stakeholders focusing on operational performance and issues which are captured in an action plan which considers forward looking strategy and future customer needs. The stakeholder management approach effectively controls the business partnership between Procurement and relevant stakeholder groups. Key data is held in one place with issues regularly documented and well communicated within the Procurement function and if relevant the organisation. Internal Service Level Agreements (SLAs) exist between Procurement and key stakeholders.	There is a set schedule with stakeholders of business and strategic reviews which are held at least quarterly. Success is measured against plans and customer satisfaction surveys. A true partnership exists between Procurement and stakeholder groups based on visibility and understanding of each other's needs, constraints and cost drivers. 360 degree reviews are undertaken annually with key suppliers.

Category management delivers the category strategy for each discrete grouping of products and services and defines the specific approaches at whichever level purchases are grouped.

Description

This profile is applicable globally, regionally and locally at the category level, and is heavily related to the strategy determined during the strategic sourcing process. It is made up of the elements required to successfully deliver the category strategy, supporting a focused and well communicated view of spend, approach and on-going interaction with procurement stakeholders and the supply base.

Context

The impact of effective category management is operationally broad, and its importance cannot be overestimated. The approach makes relevant procurement representatives and stakeholders the expert in a group, or sub-group, of products, and gives them responsibility for the on-going maintenance of supply and delivery of the category strategy. Truly effective category management often unlocks additional benefits not realised by basic operational purchasing, allowing innovation and communication to flourish, and often enhances the benefits of discrete product areas when considered together as a category.

Glossary

PPV

Abbreviation for Purchase Price Variance which is the difference between the actual price paid to buy an item and its standard price, multiplied by the actual number of units purchased. A positive variance means that actual costs have increased, and a negative variance means that actual costs have declined.

SRM

Abbreviation for Supplier Relationship Management - the process by which key supplier relationships are managed and also often applied to software that is used to support these processes.

B3 Elements	Competency	Proficiency	Mastery
B3.1 Spend analysis	Total organisational spend is understood. Stakeholders are identified and engaged in the process. Spend by supplier is understood. Spend by category is understood.	Expenditure trends are identified and understood. Future requirements and demand are identified. There is detailed knowledge of spend category and sub-category. There is detailed understanding of the factors which influence Purchase Price Variance (PPV).	Drivers for expenditure trends and demand are understood. There is a detailed understanding of spend segmentation. There is consistent multi-level category/ commodity code structure. There is regular reporting of PPV synchronised to the budget cycle.
B3.2 Category segmentation and approach	Supplier segmentation takes account of level of relationship, spend and risk. Supply market research is conducted. There is a good knowledge of current suppliers.	Segmentation take account of supply market conditions and strategic importance. Supply market reviews are conducted. There is a good understanding of technical specifications. There is regular assessment of current approach and cost drivers and good practices are captured. Potential local circumstances are considered.	Segmentation takes account of a wide range of success criteria such as innovation, flexibility, low-cost sourcing, integration and market conditions. Regular market analysis is conducted, providing a comprehensive knowledge of a wide range of potential suppliers and cost drivers. There is a good understanding of supply market trends. Good practices and actions are captured in a maturity assessment encompassing the types of strategy and tactics developed at local and regional levels.

B3.3 Category strategies	Category strategies are available for all key purchases and are aligned to global policy. Continuity of supply is included for major suppliers. The category strategy is signed off by Procurement. Operational plans exist to deploy the agreed category strategy, including identifying the implementation team as well as broad timescales for deployment.	Category strategies are available for at least 90% of spend and are aligned to global policy, with alternative supply arrangements in place. Continuity of supply is included within all category strategies. The category strategy is developed with and signed off by relevant stakeholders. The strategic focus is on balancing cost with the broad supply chain objectives and service level delivery.	Clear, comprehensive, well documented category strategies are available for all direct and non-direct materials and services and are aligned to global policy. Business risk is shared fully with the suppliers. Implementation processes are defined and documented. Strategies can be global, regional or local based upon supply market assessment; focus is on maximising customer value. Development opportunities are captured and signed off by Senior Management with multi-functional input.
B3.4 Stakeholder engagement	Stakeholders are identified. Business leadership is involved in financial control of external spend. The organisation enforces sourcing strategies by modifying IT systems.	Key stakeholders are regularly engaged in the process. Regular cross-functional team meetings giving pro-active advice on solving business problems, with customer requirements a priority. Business leadership understands the value of procurement, is fully supportive of plans and involves Procurement in business issues. Key stakeholders input into the sourcing strategy.	Key stakeholders needs and wants are identified as part of a process focused initiative. Cross-functional teams are involved in strategic sourcing and non-procurement activities, integrating team goals with business needs. Business leadership is actively involved in Supplier Relationship Management (SRM) as a partnership to build and maintain the supply base. Stakeholders are fully involved in changes to sourcing strategies with the process led and facilitated by procurement.

(continued on next page)

B3 Elements	Competency	Proficiency	Mastery
B3.5 Supplier base optimisation	There is a supplier rationalisation plan in place. Successful suppliers are retained for future purchases with some level of competitive bidding.	Consolidated purchasing is in place across the company for significant purchases. A plan exists with achievable targets for supplier optimisation. Alliances with key suppliers are in place where appropriate, for example product development or technology. The Procurement group continuously seek new suppliers that can introduce innovation to drive competitive edge.	Success in consolidation and supply base optimisation is reviewed regularly. Consortium purchasing is considered where appropriate. Well structured, long-term partnerships are established in all appropriate areas. Supplier complacency is averted by regular, open market, structured testing.
B3.6 Product or service specification	Specifications include functional requirements. Current products and services are assessed based on customer pressure. A structure is in place to capture and communicate requirements.	Cross-functional specification teams exist including procurement representation. A supplier assessment methodology is fully adopted with initial contracting in line with category strategies and procurement agenda. A detailed communication strategy is in place for major product or service developments. Specification is performance focused. Specification is value engineering based.	Cross-functional specification teams are fully integrated into the organisation. There is a consistent approach to specifications, with clear technological direction and understanding of market vs. requirements exists. Clear, unambiguous supplier evaluation criteria are updated regularly. There is evidence that standardisation and supply base rationalisation has continuously reduced complexity and costs. Decisions are based on a combination of total cost management, target costing and activity based costing as appropriate.

B3.7 Data standardisation	There is a process in place to identify duplicate and obsolete entries in the vendor masters. Data ownership is defined. Procurement category/commodity coding is established.	There are common vendor masters across the business unit. There are common part masters across the business unit. Data is owned and maintained by the Procurement function. Procurement category/commodity coding is universally applied across the organisation.	There are integrated vendor masters without duplicate entries across the organisation. There are integrated item masters without duplicate entries across the organisation. Data is owned and maintained by the Procurement function, and by a dedicated manager or team depending on volume and frequency of maintenance. There is consistent multi-level category/commodity code structure.

Using a strategic sourcing approach ensures that goods and services are sourced from the most appropriate suppliers at highly competitive prices and terms.

Description

This profile is applicable at the local, regional or global level. The seven step strategic sourcing approach optimises and aligns the supplier base to the company's requirements. In conjunction with this it optimises the spend in each category and manages company risk. This is done through defining and executing a procurement strategy for each category.

Context

The impact of strategic sourcing can be felt on two levels: operational and financial. Operationally, an effective process will ensure that there is clarity in the expectations of supplier and customer for service and quality aspects. Financially, an effective sourcing strategy should see lower cost benefits by the use of common suppliers across a broad geographic area. A good sourcing strategy will also include elements like supply risk/contingency planning, identifying (and nurturing) alternative sources/technologies. It may initiate changes in inbound supply processes, product quality, production methods and stockholding levels/costs.

Glossary

RFI

Abbreviation for Request For Information, used at the start of a sourcing process to establish the suitability of potential suppliers on the long list, which can also be known as a prequalification questionnaire. This briefly outlines the requirements and asks suppliers if they are able and willing to quote for these requirements and to give information to prepare a shortlist.

RFP

Abbreviation for Request For Proposal, used at the tendering part of the sourcing process to formalise each supplier's proposal for meeting the company's requirements. The RFP process brings structure to the procurement decision and allows the risks and benefits to be identified clearly upfront. The RFP may dictate to varying degrees the exact structure and format of the supplier's response. The creativity and innovation that suppliers choose to build into their proposals may be used to judge supplier proposals against each other, at the risk of failing to capture consistent information between bidders and thus hampering the decision making process. Effective RFPs typically reflect the strategy and short/long-term business objectives, providing detailed insight into which suppliers will be able to offer a matching perspective.

RFQ

Abbreviation for Request For Quotation, used at the tendering part of the sourcing process to establish each suppliers best price for meeting the company's requirements. An RFQ typically involves more than the price per item. Information like payment terms, quality level per item or contract length can be requested during the bidding process. The suppliers have to return the bidding by a set date and time to be considered for an award. Discussions may be held on the bids (often to clarify technical capabilities or to note errors in a proposal). The bid does not have to mean the end of the bidding. Multiple rounds can follow or even a Reverse Auction can follow to generate the best market price.

Using a strategic sourcing approach ensures that goods and services are sourced from the most appropriate suppliers at highly competitive prices and terms.

eRFX

Abbreviation for electronic Request For Information/Proposal/Quotation. Electronic sourcing (eSourcing) systems are now often used to speed up and add transparency to the sourcing process. These systems allow both the potential suppliers and the buyer to log in to enter and view their bids.

Reverse Auction

In a reverse auction, sellers compete to obtain business, and prices typically decrease over time. These are usually conducted electronically online as the price negotiation part of a strategic sourcing process. A reverse auction (also called procurement auction, e-auction, sourcing event, e-sourcing or eRA) enables quoting to be performed in real-time via the Internet. This results in dynamic bidding and helps to achieve rapid downward price pressure that is not normally attainable using traditional static paper based bidding processes.

Terms & conditions

The legal terms and conditions of purchase, often attached to standard orders or tenders by the buyer.

B4 Elements	Competency	Proficiency	Mastery
B4.1 Category level spend analysis	Total acquisition cost across each category is understood. Historical data is complete and standardised across the organisation for each category.	Category level spend analysis is used to define opportunities in conjunction with business need. Whole life cost is implemented where appropriate. Activity based costing concepts are applied.	Opportunities to satisfy the business need have been evaluated taking into account internal and external influences, risks and issues and total cost of ownership. Total supply chain costs are integrated into value creation opportunities. Total supply chain costs are used to enable cost based decisions.
B4.2 Determine business requirements	Business requirements are based on historical data, market understanding and Procurement function experience. Business requirements are linked to the strategy.	A concerted effort is made to engage stakeholders and review the previous year in terms of supplier and business performance. Business requirements include service specification and end user or customer need.	Users and key stakeholders are engaged to understand current supplier performance, detailed future demand profile and agreed future spend baseline. There is broad buy-in from business users to the sourcing project and on-going support as the project progresses. The revised baseline spend for forward periods is defined, presented to and signed-off by the project team, including any specification changes. Emerging constraints and any scope impact are reviewed regularly.

B4 Elements	Competency	Proficiency	Mastery
B4.3 Conduct market analysis	External market analysis has been carried out. Potential alternative suppliers are understood with relative strengths and weaknesses.	External analysis has been carried out using a defined set of relevant tools. The supply market is understood with cost and non-cost drivers in the marketplace captured and documented. All relevant potential suppliers will be involved due to the thoroughness of the process.	Cost implications are considered when analysing opportunities to present to stakeholders. In-depth knowledge has been developed of the category's supply market, supply chain structure and economics. There is a strong understanding of the supply market's value drivers. Total market definition is captured before creating a procurement strategy.
B4.4 Develop category strategy	The strategy includes historical and forecast requirements and previous supplier performance on delivery, quality and service levels. The category strategy defines the approach to the market that will be undertaken, considering the nature of the goods or service. Additional information for development of the strategy is derived from input from key stakeholders (e.g. Users, Quality, Manufacturing, Marketing).	The strategy is developed with key stakeholders, most likely through a category sourcing team, and signed off by all budget holders. The category strategy defines the criteria that will be used to select the supplier. Category strategies are updated in line with market conditions.	The results of the category strategy are tracked and visible to all stakeholders. All aspects of supplier selection, appointment and management have been considered and agreed with key internal stakeholders. The resulting strategy is fully appropriate to the nature of the category.

B4.5 Select suppliers and negotiate	The approach to market involves a range of standardised communication templates (Request For Information, Proposal and Quotation - RFI, RFP and RFQ). Evaluation criteria are defined and stakeholders approve recommendations made. The supplier selection process is defined. There are formalised parameters for supplier selection including: cost, quality, technical, account management and financial stability. Templated agreements are in place for all categories, providing an acceptable legal framework.	The approach to the market is tailored according to the category strategy. Negotiations are planned and executed in conjunction with stakeholders, with clear roles and responsibilities. Evaluation criteria are specific to the project and signed-off with the stakeholders. There is consistent deployment of the supplier selection process regionally or divisionally. The selection process is tailored by product or service type with a high degree of cross-functional working. Standard terms and conditions and agreement templates are rigorously applied.	Negotiations are planned well in advance and conducted professionally by formally trained experts. Stakeholders are involved in feedback evaluation and supplier selection. There is consistent deployment of supplier selection across the global enterprise with standardised processes involving cross-functional teams. Agreement specific contract clauses mitigate risks and issues outside standard terms and conditions. Post contractual reviews and continuous improvement programmes are built into the contract requirements.
B4.6 Implement	An implementation plan is developed, managed and deployed to support the sourcing decision. Plans support both supplier and agreement changes. The nominated contract managers (both supplier and buyer) are responsible for implementation.	The implementation plan is actively reviewed to ensure completion. Ownership of the plan is explicit. A post implementation review is conducted including users, specific to the individual sourcing project.	Lessons from the post implementation review are routinely captured to feed back into future projects. There is a well-defined supplier on-boarding/discontinuation process which is regularly reviewed to drive continuous improvement.

B4 Elements

B4.7 Electronic sourcing tools

Competency	Proficiency	Mastery
The procurement function is aware of and has access to the tools available to automate, improve and support the sourcing process (eRFX and Reverse Auctions). The eRFX and Reverse Auctions tools have been used with understanding of the cost vs. benefit of the tools.	A clear procurement policy exists on deploying electronic tools to support the sourcing process, including: which (Reverse Auctions, eRFX), when (suitable categories/markets) and how (when to deploy and supporting strategies). A strong understanding of the risks and benefits of the tools exist. Metrics are in place to drive the appropriate adoption of electronic sourcing tools. There is suitable training on electronic sourcing tools delivered to dedicated specialist staff internally or by the service provider.	Suppliers are trained in using the tools to ensure commitment and participation. Templates are consistently re-applied across the electronic sourcing tools. Metrics are regularly reviewed with associated actions captured and tracked to drive continuous improvement.

Buy

B5 Supplier performance management

This profile covers the infrastructure in place to manage suppliers and the metrics used to evaluate success.

Description

This profile covers the organisational structure in place to successfully manage supplier performance. This includes performance metrics, supplier management teams, review processes and contract management.

Context

Poor supplier management leads to ineffective workaround processes such as high inventories to protect against erratic supplier deliveries. Inadequate contract management means that a business will fall behind in the market as it does not harness its suppliers' technical knowledge.

Glossary

Contract

The legally binding document that defines the legal terms for business between two parties. This must include details of the goods, works or services to be provided and remuneration for these. It must be mutually agreed and entered into freely by both parties. Contracts do not have to be written (unless they relate to property) but it is good practice to do so.

This profile covers the infrastructure in place to manage suppliers and the metrics used to evaluate success.

SLA

Abbreviation for a Service Level Agreement, an agreement between the supplying and receiving parties defining how the service is provided. At its most basic, an SLA details service and quality levels, but can cover every aspect of supply from cost, delivery, returns, innovation and improvement. The SLA usually forms a part of the contract between the two parties.

CoA

Abbreviation for a Certificate of Analysis, a confirmation that product conforms to attribute and analytical quality requirements and sent to the customer to negate the need for incoming inspection.

Contract management module/software package

Most major ERP software packages and full-function procurement packages have a contract management module. The module has several key functions: an electronic repository of the final contract, an alerting tool to advise when a contract expiry date is approaching (to trigger re-tendering process), and to feed the ERP with SLA metrics for continuous performance measurement.

B5 Supplier performance management

B5 Elements	Competency	Proficiency	Mastery
B5.1 Policy and approach to supplier performance management	Contracts and Service Level Agreements (SLAs) are established for the majority of material suppliers. Contract terms are aligned to sourcing strategy and there is an annual review of key elements (cost, service levels, technical support, etc.).	Both SLAs and contracts are in place and the local Procurement Manager is responsible for ensuring that suppliers perform to requirements through using KPIs. An exit strategy is clear at the time of setting up the contract. Contract extensions are considered for exceptional service, quality and cost performance. The policy is signed off at a business unit level. The 360 degree reviews are carried out with suppliers to identify relationship and contractual issues.	Local Procurement Managers and key business stakeholders input into SLA improvement process. There is full partnership between business functions and key strategic suppliers concerning annual reduction in the total cost of ownership, shared benefits and business growth. Collaboration and joint ventures are considered.
B5.2 SLA metrics	All appropriate internal and external stakeholders contribute to the development of the SLA. The SLA includes requirements for delivery, quality and cost management.	The SLA includes issue resolution and expected information sharing between the supplier and the site. Cost breakdowns and benchmarking KPIs ensure supplier competitiveness.	The SLA is a joint development with the preferred supplier(s) and the internal cross-functional team. The SLA defines improvement and partnership objectives, governance, innovation and joint competitive advantage opportunities.

B5 Elements	Competency	Proficiency	Mastery
B5.3 Report and monitor performance	There is an accredited supplier programme in place which includes performance validation tools such as Certificate of Analysis/Assurance (CoA) and quality audits. Suppliers receive collated local performance data on a monthly basis. Where performance falls short of the required standard, roles and responsibilities are assigned within both businesses to manage issues. Focus throughout is on price, delivery and quality failures. Suppliers maintain compliance with external standards specified in the SLA (e.g. ISO).	Supplier self-certification is validated by spot audits. Performance to SLA is monitored by relevant business functions monthly and reported to Procurement at an agreed frequency. Escalation and reporting routines are defined for issues that are not resolved on a day-to-day basis within the relevant business function. Quality issues are included in the issue resolution process. For suppliers with multi-country supply, regional performance is communicated and actions assigned where required.	Suppliers have pro-active internal quality requirements, are all accredited and held jointly responsible for final product quality outputs. Processes, roles and responsibilities are defined within the SLA to manage issues where performance falls short of required standards. Action plans are put in place for serious or long term performance issues which are monitored regularly in addition to scheduled supplier performance reviews. Where possible, joint working teams collaborate to identify and resolve potential quality issues before they become a problem. High performing suppliers are recognised within the customer's business and best practices are shared with the non-competing supplier base.
B5.4 Issue resolution	Issue resolution activity takes place directly between the relevant functional areas and the supplier. The Procurement team is involved and informed where appropriate.	Teams with issue resolution and supplier management responsibilities are identified within both parties. Stakeholders are educated regarding their supplier management responsibilities.	The issue resolution and supplier management approach is agreed between all stakeholders. Issue resolution/supplier management teams have defined governance and processes for escalation.

B5.5 Supplier reporting and review	There are formal, documented supplier reviews at set frequencies which are attended by Procurement and Supplier Account Managers. Supplier reviews include cost, service, quality and support. Improvement plans are established in conjunction with participants drawn from appropriate levels in both businesses.	Supplier review frequencies are tailored by supplier, attended by representatives from a number of business areas and focus on performance against the SLA and improvement plans. Supplier improvement activities are co-ordinated and have an approval process - these are documented and responsibility for maintaining these records is clearly owned. Improvement plans are based upon opportunities determined through loss analysis and supplier reviews and are jointly owned by both businesses. There is visibility of all plans by supplier at a global level.	Supplier reviews are aligned to supplier categorisation and reflect the strategic importance of the supplier. Supplier reviews include collaboration opportunities and mutual competitive advantage opportunities. Supplier/internal improvement activities are coordinated regionally and globally with an appropriate approval process. Plans include strategic initiatives. For strategic suppliers appropriate reviews are undertaken at a senior management level on both sides.
B5.6 Contract register and management	All contracts have a defined owner. There is a contract register in place. Operational contract performance managed by the functional team which requires the products or services.	Contracts are in place for all items and are aligned to regional and global strategies. The Procurement team is responsible for reviewing contracts and a process is in place. There is a central electronic contract register which is held at a regional level. All regional contracts have local variations but are regionally owned.	Contracts are in place which reflect the strategy for the item (e.g. a globally sourced item will have a global contract). Where a single contract is not possible for legal reasons there is an agreed 'memorandum of understanding' in place. Stakeholders are defined for each contract and involved in the review process. There is an electronic global contract register (typically a part of a contract management module/software package) and there is a process in place for regular review. The contract register is managed around new contract tender lead-times.

This profile looks at the mechanisms in place to improve the service provided by Procurement and the wider inbound supply chain to the organisation.

Description

The profile of Supply Development covers the way in which the Procurement function provides support to the organisation in terms of cost reduction, quality and leveraging supplier services.

Context

Robust supply development activity ensures that an organisation uses its assets effectively through including procurement in business activities. Unless Procurement can demonstrate added value, they are relegated to managing the purchasing process and the organisation will not benefit from improved efficiencies or supplier knowledge.

Glossary

Value analysis

Examination of each procurement item to ascertain its total cost of acquisition, maintenance, and usage over its useful life and, wherever feasible, to replace it with a more cost effective substitute.

OTIF

Abbreviation for deliveries being 'On Time In Full'. This is a common metric to measure the delivery element of a supplier's performance.

SLA

Abbreviation for a Service Level Agreement, an agreement between the supplying and receiving parties defining how the service is provided. At its most basic, an SLA details service and quality levels, but can cover every aspect of supply from cost, delivery, returns, innovation and improvement. The SLA usually forms a part of the contract between the two parties.

Open book

A term used where a supplier allows full visibility of its financial information related to the customer's account. Often used for outsourced contracts, the customer is able to audit the supplier's costs and margins to assess that they are compatible with the terms of the contract.

NPD

Abbreviation for New Product Development, the process by which new products or services are developed by the organisation for its customers. Its relevance to Procurement is the extent the function and key suppliers are involved in this process to leverage all available knowledge.

This profile looks at the mechanisms in place to improve the service provided by Procurement and the wider inbound supply chain to the organisation.

NPI

Abbreviation for New Product Introduction, the process by which new products or services are introduced. This includes the planning of new products with suppliers and any phase-in phase-out planning with products that are being replaced and ramp up volume planning.

Gap analysis

Reviewing results versus a pre-assigned target, often completing pareto analysis to highlight the biggest issues.

B6 Elements	Competency	Proficiency	Mastery
B6.1 Introduction of innovation in goods and services	Tenders regularly require evidence of supplier innovation.	Preferred suppliers are involved in setting specifications for the elements of a finished product which they supply. There is a recognised process for sharing, assessing and implementing supplier-initiated innovative proposals. Suppliers are recognised at senior executive level as contributors to the competitive edge of the company and those that make the most difference are rewarded with more business, where appropriate.	There is a category management approach in place which involves key suppliers from the outset. Designs are shared between the customer and preferred supplier - there may be integration of the design systems. There are regular supplier forums for innovation and market analysis sharing. Opportunities are sought for innovative business relationships to drive mutual benefits (e.g. gainshare or joint ventures).
B6.2 Supply improvement planning	Meetings are held with suppliers to discuss improvements when problems occur. Suppliers have performance targets (typically across cost, supply and quality areas) which are regularly communicated and discussed. Cost reduction programmes are in place.	The Procurement team meets suppliers regularly to proactively identify improvement opportunities. There is transparency of information between suppliers and buyers to drive collaboration. Cost reduction programmes are aligned to sourcing strategies. Performance targets are jointly owned and responsibility of achieving them is shared.	Multi-functional teams which include suppliers meet regularly to review performance and identify areas for improvement. For weaker performing suppliers, a supplier development programme is in place which has visibility across both businesses. For high performing suppliers, a peer-to-peer collaborative approach is undertaken so that both parties can learn and grow from each other. There is a multi-tiered supplier certification/accreditation programme in place.

B6 Elements	Competency	Proficiency	Mastery
			Cost reduction and total cost management are integral parts of supply development programmes with both parties expected to share in the benefits. Real-time access between supplier and buyer for demand planning and fulfilment information.
B6.3 Reviewing/ updating	Contractual improvement targets are updated at least annually. Reviews take place at least annually. Contractual improvement targets are updated based on a combination of business requirements and demonstrated capability.	Supply review is an internal process but is communicated to suppliers who also provide objective input to the review prior to finalisation. Reviews include representation from the wider supply chain. Supplier performance is included in the review and their targets are also updated as a result. Improvement targets are communicated to the wider supply chain. The review includes discussion of potential supply risks and remedies as well as strategy. A named individual is responsible for owning the review and ensuring the updates are communicated. This is independent of the Supply Review.	Strategic supply reviews take place at least every quarter and involve multi-functional teams – a primary goal is to ensure alignment to regional and global plans. High-performing preferred suppliers are engaged at several stages in the review process to leverage their insight and capabilities. Improvements are evaluated based on shared benefits between the supplier and the buyer. Targets are analysed and updated prior to communication to the wider business.

B6.4 Measurement and delivery of benefits	The Procurement team is measuring and reporting the delivery of benefits against the plan. The Procurement team analyses conformance to targets at least annually.	Benefits are defined and validated by finance and budget holders. Gaps in achieving targets are discussed at regular reviews and action plans put in place to achieve them. Progress towards targets is tracked and communicated within the supply chain. There is an agreed approach to sharing benefits with suppliers where appropriate.	A formal improvement programme is in place which includes multi-functional teams and suppliers working to agreed targets. Measurement is carried out by a dedicated (and impartial) supply chain resource. Gap analysis is part of the executive level review of the business.
B6.5 Partnering and outsourcing	The 'make/buy' question is considered when a contract is due to expire. Outsourcing of non-core services such as catering and cleaning is considered to established third parties who specialise in these areas. Suppliers are required to provide evidence of partnering and 'open book' contracts. A detailed business case is a pre-requisite for any partnering or outsourcing strategy.	Suppliers of outsourced categories are reviewed at least annually to determine whether financial, quality and efficiency targets have been met. Tenders require the supplier to provide evidence of experience of long term relationships. All contracts allow for transparency of appropriate information and subsequent corrections to contractual formulae. Where relevant, year-on-year cost reductions (typically via operational efficiencies) are built into the contract.	There is a review of the way in which products and services are provided via refresh of the category strategies and an organisational spend review at regular intervals. Multi-functional teams consider external options for supply as a matter of course. Long term partnerships exist with suppliers in key outsourced categories where there is a cost, quality or efficiency benefit and suppliers are selected where this is demonstrated experience. Advanced contractual arrangements are in place that benefit both parties for short, medium and long-term achievements. Arrangements allow for flexing of service up or down within agreed parameters without extensive contractual renegotiation.

B7 Operational purchasing

Operational purchasing covers the typical day-to-day purchasing activities in support of the business.

Description
The profile of Supply Development covers the way in which the Procurement function provides support to the organisation in terms of cost reduction, quality and leveraging supplier services.

Context
Whilst there may be initial and on-going category sourcing strategies in place, there are still the day-to-day purchasing tasks to be performed. Areas such as chasing suppliers for deliveries, managing defective parts returns and handling invoice miss-matches are typical examples. The challenge is to automate as many of the processes as possible so that the remaining tasks are more added-value as opposed to being merely reactive to events or situations.

Glossary

SLA

Abbreviation for a Service Level Agreement, an agreement between the supplying and receiving parties defining how the service is provided. At its most basic, an SLA details service and quality levels, but can cover every aspect of supply from cost, delivery, returns, innovation and improvement. The SLA usually forms a part of the contract between the two parties.

Payment - self-billing

In some manufacturing businesses it is possible to link payments to suppliers based on production volumes. For example, a car has 2 headlights, so a single-sourced headlight supplier could be paid by the number of cars that were built (@ 2 headlamps per car) not on the number of headlights actually delivered by the supplier. So the supplier needs only to verify proposed payment each month and not to submit their own invoices. This requires accurate bills-of-material, lean supply practices and minimal inventory losses/damage to be a viable payment process.

Purchase-to-pay (P2P) systems

Purchase-to-pay, often abbreviated to P2P, refers to the business processes that cover activities of requesting (requisitioning), purchasing, receiving, paying for and accounting for goods and services. Although it does not necessarily refer directly to the application of technology to the purchasing process, it is most often used in relation to applications like e-procurement and ERP purchasing and payment modules.

Operational purchasing covers the typical day-to-day purchasing activities in support of the business.

EDI

Electronic Data Interchange (EDI) refers to the structured transmission of data between organisations by electronic means. Or, more precisely, 'the computer-to-computer interchange of strictly formatted messages that represent documents other than monetary instruments. Human intervention in the processing of a received message is typically intended only for error conditions.'

MRP

Abbreviation for Materials Requirement Plan; this is a time-phased plan of materials requirements, generated through analysing the production plan and applying the BOM (bill-of-material) for each item or SKU (stock-keeping unit). When the current stock levels, required safety stock levels, minimum order quantities and order lead times of each material item is taken into account, the optimal time to order each item is calculated.

Terms and conditions

The legal terms and conditions of purchase, often attached to standard orders or tenders by the buyer.

ERP

Enterprise Resource Planning. A system that is used to manage and coordinate all the resources, information, and functions of a business.

B7 Elements	Competency	Proficiency	Mastery
B7.1 Order systems	There is an integrated ordering system along the internal supply chain. Automatic call-off orders are sent to suppliers by fax/email/internet for direct materials. There is efficient handling of one-off orders using an e-procurement system typically for pre-production parts and indirect goods and services. Fraud opportunity is reduced through appropriate segregation of duties.	Either Electronic Data Interchange (EDI) or internet based systems are used for call-offs with key suppliers. A workflow-driven e-procurement system is used across the business for Indirects.	Fully integrated e-procurement and Purchase-to-Pay (P2P) systems are used.
B7.2 Returns process	Quality issues are managed directly by the Quality function with liaison between the Material Planner and suppliers to ensure stock replenishment of the returned material. There is a defined process to inform the buyer of rejection. For major quality issues an emergency notification system is in place.	The buyer has overall responsibility for quality performance of supplier. The supplier guarantees that all production lots produced at the same time as the rejected material are checked before shipment. The Quality function uses a well-defined process to help determine the cause of return material and manage any resulting actions.	Stock replenishment (if required) is organised by the supplier once the material is rejected and communicated to the Material Planner. All roles and responsibilities are stated in the Service Level Agreement (SLA). Failures feed into KPI reporting. Full IT systems support is in place to track and trace returns, resupplied items and to provide supplier statistics.

B7.3 Procurement controls	Purchasing processes and controls are in place. Authorisation limits are in place. Purchase controls are integrated into functional operating procedures with consistent application across sites. Standardised purchase order terms and conditions are applied rigorously.	Differentiated purchasing processes and controls are dependent on procurement category and level of spend. Orders are system generated with online checking against agreed spend limits and an electronic authorisation process that is fully auditable. Standardised purchase order terms and conditions are adapted to suit contract requirements via a controlled process.	Authorised signatories are communicated to suppliers. Procedures are in place to ensure an order can only proceed with appropriate sign-off.
B7.4 Invoice processes	All suppliers are fully informed of invoice processes and on information requirements at supplier initiation stage by buyer. There is a defined process for addressing supplier invoice queries with appropriate involvement from the buyer.	There is extensive use of consolidated and itemised invoices from high volume suppliers to reduce processing and payment authorisation. Where needed, internal invoice approval processes by budget holders is via workflow with auto chasing mechanisms to ensure timely processing. Procurement cards are implemented for appropriate low-value spend.	An internet portal is used for suppliers to upload invoices and test their acceptance criteria before e-submission. Suppliers are able to view invoice progress via an internet portal. A payment 'self-billing' process is used where appropriate.
B7.5 Payment terms	The company's standard payment terms are deployed with only a few exceptions signed-off by the Finance Director. There is internal commitment to pay on time to suppliers who have met goods/services quality and timeliness on paperwork submission. The company's standard payments terms are aligned to the company's commercial strategy.	The company's standard payments terms are consistently deployed unless favourable discounts are offered for early settlement. The Finance team perform cash flow cost/benefit analysis of taking up negotiated early settlement based on real-time view.	Whilst standard payments terms are typically used, proactive dialogue with major suppliers on short/medium term changes in payment terms are based on appropriate factors including cost of capital, cash flow projections and investment scenarios. Staged payments are embedded for all appropriate capital requirements and linked to verifiable performance. A supply chain finance solution is available to suppliers.

(continued on next page)

B7 Elements

B7.6 Purchase -to-pay systems

Competency	Proficiency	Mastery
The P2P process is systemised. Reporting by budget code, supplier and spend category is available. An automated requisition approval process is in place (e.g. via an email workflow mechanism). An e-procurement system is used for Indirects.	A robust P2P system is in place using workflow for requisition and Purchase Order (PO) sign-off based on delegated levels. Real-time integration with corporate finance system exists. Reporting also shows commitment code. Full category and supplier spend analysis capabilities are present.	The P2P system works in real-time with the ERP/Finance system. Comprehensive reporting and alerting capabilities are exploited to manage commitments, exceptions and stakeholder budgets. An internet portal is used for suppliers to upload information and/or documents and to review proposed payments.

Indirect procurement covers the ordering and control processes for indirect goods and services.

Description

This typically includes a requisitioning process that allows users to request the goods and services that they need, supported by the appropriate ordering and control processes. Indirect categories typically include the indirect spend on goods and services (e.g. cars, stationery, photocopiers, leased buildings, facilities management, insurance).

Context

In many businesses the direct materials - the items that go directly into the products made - are well controlled. Outside of these needs, the indirects often receive less focused procurement involvement even though the actual expenditure can be significant. This profile explores how the procurement team engages with stakeholders and suppliers for the indirect expenditure.

Glossary

SLA

Abbreviation for a Service Level Agreement, an agreement between the supplying and receiving parties defining how the service is provided. At its most basic, an SLA details service and quality levels, but can cover every aspect

Indirect procurement covers the ordering and control processes for indirect goods and services.

of supply from cost, delivery, returns, innovation and improvement. The SLA usually forms a part of the contract between the two parties.

Maverick spend

The term 'maverick' is used to describe purchase orders not placed with preferred suppliers or for products/services outside of the agreed specifications. This is typically likely for indirect spend where users have a preference to use local suppliers rather than the company's regional/national suppliers or to specify more expensive products rather than those already approved for use via the e-catalogues (e.g. use local recruitment company v contracted national temporary labour provider, 100gsm A4 paper v standard 80gsm, roller ball pens v standard biros etc.). Apart from losing leverage with contracted suppliers there can be health & safety or other implications if products ordered are not in line with company specifications.

Purchase-to-pay (P2P) systems

Purchase-to-pay, often abbreviated to P2P, refers to the business processes that cover activities of requesting (requisitioning), purchasing, receiving, paying for and accounting for goods and services. Although it does not necessarily refer directly to the application of technology to the purchasing process, it is most often used in relation to applications like e-procurement and ERP purchasing and payment modules.

E-cataloguing

E-procurement and P2P systems allow the creating of electronic catalogues of products and, potentially, services. These online catalogues enable company users to search, identify and select pre-agreed products/services for which the Procurement organisation has negotiated prices and specifications. Apart from making the requisitioning and ordering process easy, it also controls where and on what, the company's money is spent.

B8 Elements	Competency	Proficiency	Mastery
B8.1 Requisitioning process	The e-procurement system enables dispersed users to raise requisitions and have them approved online by line management. Main repeat type items (e.g. stationery & IT consumables) have been catalogued on system to aid users and channel spend.	The requisitioning module is integrated to the Purchase-to-Pay (P2P) system. Approvals are managed by a workflow process which can be used by smartphone as well as email. Users can interrogate the system to find requisition status. Emergency order placement is available online and offline for major sites via predetermined 24 hour third party service arrangements with full financial auditing controls in place. All main indirect spend areas are covered by e-catalogues or online links to preferred suppliers.	Workflow for approvals alerts users for overdue tasks. There is full reporting on requisition status through to order placement. A documented Servicer Level Agreement (SLA) is in place for emergency order placement.
B8.2 Indirects ordering process	After requisitioning approval, where items are selected from pre-agreed e-catalogues, the e-procurement system automatically generates a purchase order and issues it to the preferred supplier(s) without Procurement's intervention.	Over 80% of approved requisitions can be fulfilled by auto-generation of purchase orders which are issued to contracted suppliers covering most products and often used services (e.g. temporary labour). Utilities, rent/rates and corporate services are managed via appropriate ordering, payment and audit mechanisms. Full reporting capability is available on ordering process including time to order for non-automated needs.	Over 95% of indirect requirements are fulfilled by the e-procurement/P2P system. There is a high functionality requisitioning/ordering process for complex services following collaboration with preferred suppliers to agree hourly/day rates, parameters of work, mileage rates etc.

B8.3 Non-contract spend management	For requisitions of items or services not covered by the system, Procurement receives a 'requirements' list of requirements and these are automatically allocated to buyers based on category codes entered by users. A system workflow is in place for approval of requisitions.	The Procurement team has early sight of pre-authorised requisitions as well as receiving system-generated action lists based on category allocation. New product and service requirements are assessed for blanket order/cataloguing potential to automate subsequent needs.	All raised requisitions with non-contract items/suppliers are immediately e-alerted to Procurement's category buyer for review (expand current supplier scope, find new supplier etc.) to speed up fulfilment and maximise buying leverage. Proactive Procurement involvement is evident, with user stakeholders for potential novel requirements to assess supply market options.
B8.4 Maverick spend/contract compliance	The e-procurement/P2P system identifies spend outside of current contractual or non - contractual arrangements. No more than 20% of spend is identified as 'maverick' and is reported at least quarterly. The Procurement team contacts user departments to re-educate them on the need to use existing suppliers/products and/or to understand the reason why existing arrangements are unsuitable. Fraud loops are kept under constant surveillance.	Maverick spend is less than 10%. Stakeholder engagement is done proactively to drive compliance and to explore new requirements. Users have intranet access to supplier catalogues, ordering process and a help desk to make compliance easier. Senior management give visible policy and operational support to reduce maverick activity. Monthly reporting of maverick spend leads to stakeholder reviews.	Maverick spend is less than 3%, typically driven by immediacy of need rather than avoidance of current arrangements. Users are given broad support in use of system, processes and supplier information as well as a help desk. The P2P system immediately generates alerts for any likely maverick activity to avert ordering outside existing contractual and non-contractual agreements. There is full management buy-in to the use of the P2P system and the contractual arrangements; non-compliance is potentially treated as a disciplinary matter. Preferred suppliers actively support only the approved ordering methods and report on attempts to circumvent correct ordering routines.

B9 Capital Procurement

Capital procurement covers the procurement processes specifically for capital expenditure and projects (e.g. IT infrastructure, plant and equipment and building refurbishment).

Description

Capital procurement covers the procurement processes specifically for capital expenditure and projects (e.g. IT infrastructure, plant and equipment and building refurbishment).

Context

In many businesses the direct materials - the items that go directly into the products made - are well controlled. Outside of these needs, indirects such as capital projects often receive less focused procurement involvement even though the actual expenditure can be significant. This profile explores how the procurement team engages with stakeholders and suppliers for capital expenditure.

Glossary

SLA

Abbreviation for a Service Level Agreement, an agreement between the supplying and receiving parties defining how the service is provided. At its most basic, an SLA details service and quality levels, but can cover every aspect of supply from cost, delivery, returns, innovation and improvement. The SLA usually forms a part of the contract between the two parties.

TCO

Abbreviation for Total Cost of Ownership which allows Procurement to make more informed financial decisions about the product or service that offers the best value for money over the life of the product or service. Rather than just looking at the purchase price, TCO looks at the complete cost from purchase to disposal. It adds to the initial purchase price other costs expected to be incurred during the life, such as service, repair, utility costs and insurance.

B9 Elements	Competency	Proficiency	Mastery
B9.1 Capital expenditure planning	The Procurement team are aware of CapEx plans for the year and potential timings of projects. Stakeholders engage with Procurement at an early stage to get input/guidance on contractual and commercial matters including assessing lead-times.	The Procurement team are involved in the annual CapEx project sign-off meeting to gain insight into areas of spend and potential 'bundling' of needs and any synergies with existing supplier/contractor base. The Procurement team are represented at all major CapEx project planning meetings. The Procurement team are engaged on all commercial/contractual matters.	The Procurement team input into the long-term budget planning. Key suppliers are involved in the planning of new projects at an early stage. Innovative use of funding is considered at an early stage.
B9.2 Capital expenditure specification development	The Procurement team provides guidance to stakeholders on developing performance specifications and avoiding closing supply options too early.	The Procurement team influences specifications to ensure open competition is possible. The Procurement team sign-off specifications as appropriate for market competition and supply.	The Procurement team is part of the cross-functional team that jointly develops most appropriate specifications to meet all the business's needs (technical, strategic, operational, commercial). Value mapping and cost/benefit analysis are conducted by Procurement on elements of contractual terms or bundle options.

B9.3 Capital expenditure contract development

The Procurement team are involved in negotiations; structuring the terms and conditions and issuing final contract for major requirements as resources allow. Standard CapEx contract templates are in existence and approved by legal team. The Procurement team takes the lead in commercial aspects of major contracts and provides guidance for other contracts.	The Procurement team has overall responsibility for structure and comprehensiveness of the contract. Novel aspects of the contract promptly supported by the legal team. The Procurement team works closely with stakeholders on setting metrics in the SLA aspects of the contract. A stage payments approach is always considered for complex projects, provided that a bankers guarantee or alternative security is in place. The majority of contracts are based on CapEx contract templates.	There is a strong focus on stage payments, title, retention and after-sales support costs/support. The existing range of CapEx contract templates are reviewed annually. The Procurement team are responsible for achieving optimum terms and conditions at the right price based on Total Cost of Ownership (TCO) analysis over an appropriate time period.

Buy

B10 Sustainability in sourcing

Sustainable sourcing ensures that materials, products and suppliers are environmentally managed such that costs and risks to future supply are minimised, and company reputation is protected and enhanced within the supply chain.

Description

This profile applies to the appropriate function whether local, regional or global to understand how strategies are developed and managed for the site subject to review.

- Assessment of environmental impacts during the design phase for new products
- Consideration of environmental, social and ethical aspects of sourcing decisions
- Positive engagement with suppliers to audit and improve the impacts of their operations

Context

Typically over 80% of the environmental impact of any product is fixed during the design stages. Early consideration of the full lifecycle of the product and the materials used to manufacture, package and transport it will enable these impacts to be minimised. This in turn offers opportunities to reduce costs, simplify processes within the supply chain, and reduce operational risks. Sourcing decisions affect environmental as well as financial costs, by influencing utilisation of production assets, physical distance for transport within the supply chain and stockholdings. Suppliers are often highly visible to external stakeholders.

Careful selection and management of suppliers represents one of the major opportunities to minimise risk to the company's reputation, as well as highlighting opportunities for improving efficiency between partners in the supply chain. Building sustainability criteria into sourcing decisions has a significant influence on the impacts generated through the downstream supply chain, in Make, Deliver and Demand activities. Conversely, many issues identified in these downstream activities can only be improved or removed by medium and long term development of supplier activity.

Glossary

ISO 14001

ISO 14001 was first published as a standard in 1996 and it specifies the requirements for an organisation's environmental management system. It applies to those environmental aspects over which an organisation has control and where it can be expected to have an influence.

CSR

Abbreviation for Corporate Social Responsibility, a form of corporate self-regulation integrated into a business model. CSR policy functions as a built-in, self-regulating mechanism whereby a business monitors and ensures its active compliance with the spirit of the law, ethical standards, and international norms. CSR is a process with the aim to embrace responsibility for the company's actions and encourage a positive impact through its activities on the environment, consumers, employees, communities, stakeholders and all other members of the public sphere who may also be considered as stakeholders.

B10 Sustainability in sourcing

B10 Elements	Competency	Proficiency	Mastery
B10.1 Design for sustainability	Environmental impacts are assessed for all globally managed materials at design stage with alternative solutions evaluated. Designs are in line with ethical, environmental and Corporate Social Responsibility (CSR) policies.	Appropriate, objective metrics are used in the assessments (carbon footprint, CO_2 etc.). Environmental criteria are weighted in the final product approval process. Suppliers are engaged on specific product or service high profile sustainability concerns.	All suppliers are encouraged to propose innovative solutions with demonstrable sustainable benefits. Sustainability ideas are tracked and managed through to implementation.
B10.2 Sustainable sourcing strategy	Criteria for supplier selection include environmental, ethical and CSR aspects. Suppliers are assessed against ISO 14001. A supplier CSR audit programme is in place. CSR policy is compliant with the UN Directive on Human Rights and child exploitation.	Criteria are approved by the board, applied globally and communicated to all current and prospective suppliers. The results of the CSR audit programme are published at least annually.	Policy extends to covering all supplier tiers where appropriate and manageable. Suppliers who consistently fail to meet minimum criteria are deselected.
B10.3 Supplier development	Suppliers of all major globally managed materials and packaging have received a sustainability audit at least once and the results have been discussed with their management teams.	An action planning process is in place post-audit to monitor on-going improvement.	Key suppliers are identified and audited annually; results are presented in benchmark form with associated improvement actions identified. There is company-wide buy-in to supplier development initiatives or regulation (e.g. Forrest Stewardship Council for sustainable upstream sourcing packaging).

B10.4 Data, measurement and incentives

Data is held to ensure and prove compliance with legal and regulatory frameworks in all countries of operation.	Metrics are used to monitor and improve sustainability of materials and suppliers. Future strategy incorporates environmental, ethical and social considerations as well as economic factors.	Regulatory control is reviewed and managed at regional level. Design and Procurement staff are incentivised to improve sustainability of sourcing activities. Independent audit bodies are known, and where appropriate used to provide additional insight and monitoring capabilities.

Make

Production strategy

Detailed scheduling

Asset maintenance

Production systems

High performing teams

Sustainability in manufacturing

3 Make

The Make function focuses on ensuring that the manufacturing capability is able to operate at maximum effectiveness, that the capital equipment delivers as high a return as possible, and that service and quality expectations are routinely met or exceeded.

The Make section begins with the production strategy and scheduling process; ensuring that what a manufacturing site makes meets customer requirements and balances the costs of excessive inventory and manufacturing efficiencies.

A central tenet of manufacturing efficiency is reliability; not just ensuring the equipment has high levels of up-time, but also that changeovers are managed effectively and that manufacturing performance is monitored in the correct way. As reliability increases, variability decreases and manufacturing efficiencies rise accordingly. Machine availability is maintained by ensuring that the correct maintenance procedures are undertaken at the right time and that, as incidents such as breakdowns occur, lessons are learned to avoid recurrences.

An important foundation for manufacturing improvement is the adoption of the visual workplace; an environment where it is possible to see quickly and easily whether or not the process is in control, what work needs to be done, in what order and where it should go to next. This is achieved through the rigorous application of housekeeping standards and performance measures. A robust system for identifying problems, solutions and action plans and driving continuous improvement are also integral parts of the visual workplace.

People are also a key enabler to efficient production; not just ensuring that individuals have the skills to meet their job requirements, but also how teams are structured to support on-going development and improvement. The teams need to have the necessary range of skills to make informed decisions about their ways of working to achieve the aims of the manufacturing function. These team members should also have responsibility and accountability for the quality of their own output and, as team maturity grows, become more and more self-managing.

Where finished goods are not bought in, developing a successful manufacturing function ensures that the products, the 'public face' of a business, are of a high quality and are made at the most competitive price possible. The Make sections are designed to improve the efficiency of production operations, increase product quality and raise manufacturing yields. Effective management of manufacturing operations also improves reliability, minimises downtime, cost and waste and increases morale.

Make

M1 Production strategy

This process provides the input into the overall run strategy by challenging constraints and improving flexibility whilst configuring the production cells to best fulfil demand.

Context

Although the overall supply chain run strategy must consider factors beyond the factory such as inventory and service offering, the ability of the factory to improve responsiveness is key. Production cells must also be configured to align with the demand profile whether operating to Lean and Agile principles or segmented by product type or technology.

Glossary

Lean

Lean thinking is a methodology about simplicity, flow, visibility and value. Lean principles: (1) Specify value from the point of view of the customer. (2) Identify the value stream using mapping of physical and information flow - eliminate unnecessary non-value adding activities, reduce necessary non-value adding activities and improve value adding activities. (3) Make value flow, avoid batching and WIP. (4) Pull at the customer's rate of demand, avoid over-production. (5) Seek perfection through continual improvement.

M1 Elements	Competency	Proficiency	Mastery
M1.1 Production run strategy	The production run strategy process challenges constraints such as change-over times to enable smaller batch sizes.	The production run strategy process identifies the key constraints and enablers for greater effectiveness. Changeover reduction is an integral part of operational improvement plans.	Significant reduction in Work In Progress (WIP) has been achieved across some products through late stage differentiation. There is the ability to model different constraints to estimate benefits of run strategy changes.
M1.2 Cell strategy	Activities are in place to identify and implement approaches that are appropriate to the factory's different demand profiles.	There is good understanding of the demand characteristics that would suggest a Lean or Agile approach is appropriate. Historical and forecast demand has been analysed to identify segments and manufacturing cells have been configured and differentiated to service those segments.	There is at least an annual review of cell demand profiles to ensure complying with Lean and Agile strategies.

Make

M2 Detailed scheduling

The Detailed scheduling process allocates SKU production requirements to production resources to create an optimised shift level production schedule.

Description

This profile applies to manufacturing sites only and covers the creation and optimisation of production schedules, how they are controlled and communicated. The profile also covers how supporting schedules are developed from the final production schedule.

Context

Effective scheduling ensures weekly production requirements are satisfied whilst minimising the waste of excess production or crewing - an unrealistic schedule either results in a customer service issue or increase in manufacturing or inventory costs. The schedule is driven by the weekly SKU requirements from the Master production scheduling process.

The detailed scheduling process allocates SKU production requirements to production resources to create an optimised shift level production schedule.

Glossary

Kanban

The method of replenishment or product of material where the signal for replenishment is based upon actual usage (versus predicted usage) i.e. the downstream customer 'pulls' the product/material when required, in the quantity required.

MRP

Abbreviation for Manufacturing Resource Planning. A planning process, usually undertaken within a system, which creates production orders for resources by taking into account individual SKU routings, resource capacity and lead times.

M2 Elements	Competency	Proficiency	Mastery
M2.1 Scheduling process	Weekly production requirements are converted into a production schedule using SKU routings within the constraints of resource and material availability. Supporting department schedules are developed by Manufacturing Resource Planning (MRP) or spread sheets once the final production schedule is agreed.	Weekly production schedules are based upon agreed sequencing guidelines. There is an understanding of how orders can be moved within the firm period to optimise manufacturing costs without affecting service. Visibility of future supporting department requirements is provided by MRP and allows load levelling to ensure efficient use of resources.	Weekly or rolling daily schedules are developed in line with the production run strategy. The schedule horizon is dependent upon required revisit frequencies. Supporting schedules are subject to optimal sequencing guidelines with a focus on minimal Work In Progress (WIP). There is selective use of Kanban in place of MRP driven schedules to ensure load levelling.
M2.2 Sequencing and optimisation	Documented guidelines are used to determine production sequencing such as minimising size changes.	Sequencing guidelines (e.g. production wheels) optimise manufacturing uptime over a 2 week period. Sequencing guidelines are developed using capacity data, SKU routings and changeover times. All key sequencing parameters are held within the scheduling system.	Labour and production resource availability are parameters in a dynamic schedule. The optimisation process may suggest changes to known constraints to optimise the manufacturing cost (e.g. moving scheduled maintenance).

(continued on next page)

M2 Elements	Competency	Proficiency	Mastery
M2.3 Monitoring and exception management	Actual production versus planned is reported and reviewed weekly by production resource or product family. Plan progress is an input to the master production scheduling and supply management processes.	Daily reports of actual production against planned by SKU are reviewed to assess shortfalls. Schedule stability is measured and reported.	All exceptions are reported through a daily production review process to ensure they are highlighted, actioned and resolved. The costs of changes to the schedule are highlighted where necessary.
M2.4 Schedule development and control	A production schedule is issued weekly and frozen with respect to planned capacity for that week. The production schedule is a controlled document. The Production team ensures that all capacity data and key constraints are updated monthly.	The production schedule covers the next 2 weeks with the first week frozen and the next week in draft form for input. The schedule is issued as an output of a formal sign-off meeting with all key stakeholders. A controlled live schedule is available within the planning system.	The daily rolling schedule is available online to production, logistics and planning teams. The Production team input to a monthly capacity parameter review process that includes projections of capacity drivers (e.g. utilisation, efficiency, changeover times). The Production team provides challenge to schedules as appropriate with options based upon costed analysis.

Make

M3 Asset maintenance

Asset maintenance is the specific area of asset management that ensures equipment is available for production and the activities required to minimise downtime and cost.

Description

This profile applies to manufacturing sites only and covers the practices relating to maintaining equipment and its availability to produce. It can be divided into three sections:

- Effectiveness (what type of maintenance is used, who executes it, what procedures and tools are used to carry out the maintenance)
- Efficiency (how are maintenance, planned downtime and resources used in a cost effective manner)
- Improvement (how breakdowns are analysed to prevent reoccurrence and how key maintenance process results are reviewed to drive improvement work)

Context

At an operational level, asset maintenance ensures equipment is defect free and running so regular production output is guaranteed. However, the concepts highlighted within this profile are foundations of manufacturing excellence and the methodologies are applicable across the supply chain. Asset maintenance provides an input to the supply management process in defining what the required planned downtime will be.

Asset maintenance is the specific area of asset management that ensures equipment is available for production and the activities required to minimise downtime and cost.

Glossary

Periodic Maintenance

The routine of cleaning, inspecting, lubricating or changing parts/sub-assemblies on a pre-determined periodic basis.

Predictive Maintenance

The method of monitoring equipment to assess whether maintenance is required or the part or sub-assembly is likely to fail soon, e.g. checking electrical cabinets for heat (thermography) or gearboxes for worn bearings (vibration analysis).

OPLs

Abbreviation for One (or single) Point Lessons or visual aids that are used to highlight and share key lessons in a visual and easy to understand one page format e.g. an unguarded machine with a big cross next to it and a guarded machine with a big tick next to it, or a visual diagram of how to set-up a wrapping reel.

Job aid
A summary document or checklist to highlight the key steps, considerations and required information for a specific task e.g. key steps, part numbers and estimated time.

Common failure modes
Look to categorise failures into generic categories as well as just the specific cause in each case. These categorised failures are then reviewed on a longer-term frequency to determine trends and where the need to focus activities is. For example, using the 4M approach (Method, Machine, huMan and equipMent) might connect a number of failures (equipment, quality, reliability) to a lack of documentation or inadequate training.

CIL
Abbreviation for Clean Inspect Lubricate (CIL), the periodic maintenance tasks (see Periodic Maintenance above) that are often grouped and executed together within a system.

Intervention
Any planned stop of production equipment whether it be to carry out periodic maintenance, carry out improvement activities, train or execute changeovers (or a combination). The reason this is an element on its own is to drive the importance of pre-planning and review to maximise the effectiveness of any planned downtime, often referred to as 'pit stop' approach.

TPM
Abbreviation for Total Productive Maintenance, a methodology and toolkit that improve equipment performance through a focus on zero defects and increased employee involvement.

Asset maintenance is the specific area of asset management that ensures equipment is available for production and the activities required to minimise downtime and cost.

RCM
Abbreviation for Reliability Centred Maintenance. An equipment maintenance technique that analyses individual component failure modes to determine the most appropriate maintenance method to adopt.

OEM
Abbreviation for Original Equipment Manufacturer.

Gap analysis
Reviewing results versus a pre-assigned target, often completing pareto analysis to highlight the biggest issues.

Make

M3 Asset maintenance

M3 Elements	Competency	Proficiency	Mastery
M3.1 Strategy	The maintenance approach is driven by Original Equipment Manufacturer (OEM) recommendations. The focus is on delivering effective maintenance by reducing unplanned downtime.	The maintenance approach is driven by equipment analysis and experience. Efficient maintenance focuses on keeping planned downtime greater than unplanned. The Total Productive Maintenance (TPM) principles are well understood by all those involved in maintenance activities. Processes and analysis are in place to ensure maintenance frequencies are optimal.	The maintenance approach is driven by the total cost of maintenance including downtime, spare part and labour costs. All planned maintenance activities are reviewed post intervention to improve processes and procedures.
M3.2 Ownership	Maintenance is executed predominately by a central team alongside a few key skilled members of the operations team. Maintenance planning and performance reporting is completed at a site level.	Most operators lubricate their own equipment with plans developed to transfer other Planned Maintenance (PM) activities to operators. There is a site-wide maintenance improvement team which owns the maintenance processes and leads improvement work. Maintenance planning and performance reporting is completed at a departmental level.	Nearly all maintenance is executed by the operations team with help from central team as required. Maintenance planning and performance reporting is completed at an individual production cell level.

(continued on next page)

M3 Elements	Competency	Proficiency	Mastery
M3.3 Corrective maintenance	Separate equipment defect lists exist and abnormalities are addressed during scheduled downtime. Some general inspection standards (e.g. drives, motors) exist to help in defect identification.	A visual defect handling process is in place (T-card, red tags, online lists etc.) with a regular review of new and outstanding defects. Component-based inspection standards (e.g. belts, fasteners and bearings) are in place with visual indicators used to aid defect identification.	A documented defect handling system is in place with categorisation and prioritisation of defects linked to an intervention planning system. A One Point Lesson (OPL) approach is used to aid defect identification.
M3.4 Preventative maintenance	Fixed interval maintenance is used with specific inspection items. Some line specific maintenance procedures exist and are updated as required. Daily and weekly process cleaning requirements are documented and execution recorded.	Inspection and periodic replacement intervals are based upon individual component/assembly requirements. Fixed interval Cleaning, Inspection and Lubrication (CIL) tasks are documented with frequencies, estimated times, inspection criteria and tools. Job cards/task lists exist for 90% of regular maintenance tasks with part numbers, prework and estimated time.	A Reliability Centred Maintenance (RCM) approach is used to identify individual component failure modes and the appropriate maintenance strategy. There is extensive use of predictive and condition monitoring maintenance techniques where appropriate. Individual component requirements are reflected in the frequencies and task groupings have been optimised for minimal intervention time.

M3.5 Analysis and reporting	Major breakdowns are reviewed and preventative actions are put in place. Total line or department maintenance cost is reported and reviewed monthly with action plans in place for the top five costs. There are monthly reports on breakdown downtime as a percentage of overall downtime.	A documented template is used to ensure the right information and root cause analysis is carried out following breakdowns. Maintenance cost is known by individual equipment and is reported daily and reviewed monthly. Breakdowns (number and mean time between), maintenance costs and planned maintenance completion are reported monthly.	All breakdowns are analysed for root cause with immediate (mitigating) and preventative actions with reapplication where required. Failure mode analysis is used to highlight common failure modes across an area/site for detailed investigation. Breakdown analysis can lead to part redesign and is considered in new machine designs and/or installations. Breakdowns are reported monthly by production team with gap analysis and required actions.
M3.6 Spares management	Spares are controlled by min/max levels calculated through historic usage and value. Spare part stores are centrally located and controlled with item location dependent on category and size.	Spares levels are dictated by mix of historic usage and a calendar within a planned maintenance software (e.g. SAP PM) for periodic items. Spare part stores locations are optimised by type, size and frequency of use.	High usage items (including refurbished) are located module side and controlled by Production teams. There is pooling of spares across departments (and sites if applicable) for strategic low usage, high value spares (e.g. one holding location for multiple sites).

Production systems are those activities that maintain and improve the reliability of production performance through people, processes and tools.

Description

This profile is applicable to a factory only and applies to all aspects of the manufacturing process. This profile addresses how production performance is measured, reviewed and improved, how production environment standards are maintained, and how changes to production are managed e.g. changeovers, new materials/equipment etc.

Context

The more reliable the process, the lower the variability and the higher the output and productivity. This leads to productivity savings and greater conformance to plan. The demonstrated and predicted future reliability is used in the supply management processes.

Glossary

SMED

Abbreviation for Single Minute Exchange of Die. A Lean toolkit approach used to reduce reducing changeover time by identifying individual steps, removing non-value adding activities and streamlining the remaining value-adding activities.

5S

The name of a workplace organisation method that uses a list of five Japanese words beginning with S for its 5 phases (translated into English: sort, set, shine, standardise, sustain).

OEE

Abbreviation for Overall Equipment Effectiveness. A measure of production performance calculated by availability (%) x performance rate (%) x yield rate (%).

GMP

Abbreviation for Good Manufacturing Practice. The standards applied within sites to maintain product integrity, quality assurance and hygiene.

M4 Elements	Competency	Proficiency	Mastery
M4.1 Review and direction setting	Daily meetings are held to review key performance indicators and agree actions for the day. Formal monthly department reviews are in place to agree prioritised action plans. The line logbook is used to capture all key issues and interventions.	Handovers are used to review results and agree actions for the next shift. On-going monitoring of performance against target during the shift drives root cause analysis and planned actions. Key review meetings have documented charters which state objectives, agenda, inputs, outputs and attendees.	Weekly department reviews, review key results and gap analysis on a monthly cycle (e.g. safety week 1, quality week 2 etc.) and update the department action plan. There is a site meeting calendar that states all daily, weekly and monthly meetings down to department level. The equipment logbook is used to capture all line issues and interventions.
M4.2 Performance improvement	A monthly improvement cycle (e.g. Plan-Do-Check-Act) is used to review production reliability, downtime and waste. Performance gaps versus target are analysed in the monthly improvement cycle, and a plan to address them is determined.	Reliability reviews include multi-level pareto and root cause analysis. Reliability reviews are completed by a Process Leader together with key technical staff within the Production team.	Small group activities drive reliability improvement. Reliability reviews are led by Production team members with support from the Process Leader.
M4.3 Commissioning	There is a formal qualification process with clearly defined success criteria for safety, quality, speed, reliability and waste. New process qualification drives the development of the necessary training packages, maintenance requirements and troubleshooting guides are developed.	The documented qualification process clearly defines success criteria for acceptable levels of minor process stoppages (short stops). Qualification drives the development and updating of key process controls.	Qualification protocol includes success criteria for changeover times. Process qualification initiates a process understanding exercise to develop the appropriate quality matrices and technician training aids.

M4.4 Changeovers	The overall downtime due to changeovers is reported monthly. Changeover improvement programmes have been completed in the last year. Changeover procedures are in place and are reviewed at least annually.	Changeover loss versus target is reported monthly. Changeover improvement activities based on Single Minute Exchange of Die (SMED) have been carried out with internal and external elements identified. Procedures and checklists exist for all major changeovers and are tracked versus the target time.	All changeovers have been categorised into similar types for reporting, analysis and improvement purposes. Full SMED changeover reduction activities have been completed with all external elements executed during run time and internal elements have been streamlined.
M4.5 Workplace standards	The Leadership team understand the key elements of Good Manufacturing Practice (GMP) and have communicated the importance in the workplace. A structured housekeeping process ensures unnecessary items have been removed from the workplace.	A GMP approach is practised across all areas of the factory through production team-based activities. Audits of housekeeping standards are completed at least on a monthly basis. There are clearly assigned places for necessary equipment, tools and materials. Cleaning tasks are defined and are performed on a scheduled basis.	The 5S process has been fully implemented in all areas across the site. Cross-department audits are completed regularly to benchmark, improve and reapply standards. Required standards are clearly displayed in every area so visitors can recognise whether they are at standard or not.
M4.6 Performance measures	Machine downtime is being measured and reported. Productivity and cost is measured monthly.	Up to date measures of Overall Equipment Effectiveness (OEE) and constituent parts are recorded and displayed on most critical equipment. The number of minor process stoppages (short stops) are measured and reported. Performance measures are being formally used to drive team based shop floor continuous improvement activities.	Both OEE, the constituent measures, productivity and cost are reported monthly at a line level. Mean time between touches is measured (including both short stops and material replenishment) to support productivity improvement.
M4.7 Visual reporting	Key performance measures are visible within the department.	Short interval control charts are used to track hourly output versus targets. Key line performance indicators are displayed for each production area. The Production team's annual objectives and targets are visible.	Examples of recent improvements are displayed within each production area. Improvement team charters and plans including current are visible.

M5 High performing teams

High performing teams ensure that manufacturing processes are operated and improved as effectively and efficiently as possible by use of well-defined and managed teams.

Description

This profile applies to manufacturing sites only. The profile covers the structure, governance and mechanisms used by teams designed for high performance.

Context

Without effective teams to manage and improve manufacturing processes, output is low and unpredictable. Assigning people to tasks can only deliver so much, creating teams to own a wide-range of deliverables can guarantee quality high outputs whilst driving improvement and supporting changes.

Glossary

Gap analysis

Reviewing results versus a pre-assigned target, often completing pareto analysis to highlight the biggest issues.

Single Improvements (Kaizens)

A single implemented improvement. Normally a Kaizen (Japanese for 'improvement') refers to the one-page summary sheet which is used for sharing, re-applying and recognising improvements. Usually has the following sections: before and after (photo/diagram), what work was done, what results were achieved including quantifiable savings if possible and potential reapplication opportunities.

OPLs

Abbreviation for One (or single) Point Lessons or visual aids are used to highlight and share key lessons in a visual and easy to understand one page format e.g. an unguarded machine with a big cross next to it and a guarded machine with a big tick next to it, or a visual diagram of how to set-up a wrapping reel.

Activity boards

Visual method of displaying improvement work so progress can be monitored, shared and rewarded - can be done in Plan-Do-Check-Act format. Normally has examples of the improvement work (e.g. Kaizens), results tracking and charters.

M5 Elements	Competency	Proficiency	Mastery
M5.1 Structure	Teams are formed around operation of production resources. A Line Manager or Supervisor is in place for each team that is responsible for the execution of operational activities.	Teams are formed around key production process flows, including production resources and/or supporting processes (e.g. material movement or planning). Teams have an appointed Team Leader who is responsible for all operational activities and a line manager for strategic and organisational planning. The Line Manager acts as coach to develop the team.	Teams are self-managing with a nominated (often rotational) Team Leader with only strategic input from the Line Manager. The Line Manager acts as coach for the development of a number of Production teams.
M5.2 Direction setting	Team objectives are aligned with site objectives and reviewed annually.	The company business plan is clearly cascaded through the site then department action plan to the team objectives. The team objectives are translated into individual objectives where appropriate. A team scorecard exists to track key performance measures versus target.	Each team has a vision statement specific to their operation and aligned with the site's vision. Each team member can describe how their objectives contribute to the overall site and company objectives. Each team member has a personal scorecard to measure their performance against individual and team targets.
M5.3 Roles and responsibilities	There are defined roles and responsibilities for the team for running, troubleshooting and maintaining processes.	Specific roles exist for operational and support activities and team members are assigned to these roles on a regular frequency as appropriate.	Teams have a training owner who manages the skills matrix for the team and plans training and resources (both internal and external).

		Members of the team have functional responsibility (e.g. safety, quality, process control). Members of the team are responsible for the team meeting the requirements set by the site functional leaders.	Team members are assigned ownership for individual pieces of equipment to ensure operational and maintenance processes are tracked and improved. The team is responsible for the accuracy of material inventory records, formula cards/specifications and production reporting data.
M5.4 Self-management	The teams are responsible for operational decision making including; crewing, holiday planning, maintenance and production scheduling. The operational decision making process is supported by a clear process and guidelines.	Team members take responsibility for budgets (e.g. consumables, maintenance). Teams understand the mechanisms for decision making (principle-based, consensus, majority) and utilise them appropriately.	Where appropriate, team members are involved in succession planning, disciplinary and recruitment action planning. The team develops and owns improvement action plans with coaching from the Line Manager. The Line Manager is only required for strategic decision making, succession planning, discipline and recruitment as appropriate.
M5.5 Information	The information required to complete team roles effectively is available. All key actions are documented for reference and traceability.	All performance data to enable review, action planning and improvement activities is made available. Follow-up actions raised by the team are documented and tracked.	All functional and cost data is made available to enable operational decision making. Outstanding actions are visible to team members with review dates.
M5.6 Integration	Teams have the necessary interaction with the supporting functions required on a daily basis e.g. Quality, Planning, Technical Support.	There is team representation for projects, initiatives and functional activities.	There is team representation for off-site equipment commissioning. The Improvement teams are supported by Functional Pillar teams who provide expertise on direction, tools and coaching.

(continued on next page)

M5 Elements	Competency	Proficiency	Mastery
M5.7 Team reviews	The teams review key performance measures on a monthly basis and agree action plans. Team reviews are led by the Line Manager. Team performance against objectives is clearly visible (e.g. line boards).	Teams present key performance measures, gap analysis and action plans to the line manager on a monthly basis. Team performance against gap analysis and action plans are clearly visible.	Team reviews include a business update section from the Line Manager to provide updates on the wider business plans and potential impacts on team. Senior managers are invited to team reviews at least once a year.
M5.8 Improvement	Improvement activities are created based upon key losses and resourced by team members.	Small group activities are scheduled within the teams to address loss areas using cross-functional input as necessary. The Improvement teams develop and track key measures, perform gap analysis and update action plans. Team members share learning and improvements through One Point Lessons (OPLs) and Kaizens.	Site wide resources are included in the Improvement teams as appropriate. The Improvement teams maintain activity boards and activity plans for each session. The Production team members are represented on committees and pillar teams established to coordinate cross-factory action plans.
M5.9 Appraisals, reward mechanisms and development	There are documented performance discussions between the Line Manager and each team member at least quarterly. Each team member has a development plan detailing agreed training requirements and role preferences.	Each team member has a development plan detailing annual objectives and short and longer term career aspirations are updated annually. There are annual appraisals with reward mechanisms having performance based elements based upon team and individual measures.	Performance discussions can be held between the Team Leader and team member. There is use of peer feedback as an input to appraisals. Where possible, there are individual pay curves for each team member based upon basic citizenship, performance and skill level.

Make

M6 Sustainability in manufacturing

Sustainability in manufacturing applies to the procurement and management of manufacturing assets as well as to the efficiency of production processes and management of all resulting waste streams.

Description

This profile applies to manufacturing sites only and covers the through-life management of capital equipment, from specification through to disposal. It also covers the impacts of the manufacturing processes on the environment, including impacts on employees and local communities. Non-owned assets and plants are not in scope.

Context

Capital assets are significant investments for the business and are used for many years. It is therefore important that they are specified to operate as efficiently as possible, are correctly maintained, and their disposal or recycling is carefully considered as part of the initial investment appraisal.

Production processes may be responsible for a high proportion of the company's total environmental profile in terms of emissions and waste streams. These can have a significant impact on total operating costs, including costs of regulatory compliance. Equally, if well managed and minimised, they can help to build a positive reputation for the company and improve operating margins.

M6 Sustainability in manufacturing

Sustainability in manufacturing applies to the procurement and management of manufacturing assets as well as to the efficiency of production processes and management of all resulting waste streams.

Sustainability assessments in manufacturing operations highlight the degree of effectiveness of quality assurance, equipment maintenance and process reliability activities. Planning decisions may also have implications for sustainability in the Make set of profiles.

Make

M6 Sustainability in manufacturing

M6 Elements	Competency	Proficiency	Mastery
M6.1 Asset procurement	An environmental impact assessment is required before procurement of all capital assets.	Condition-based monitoring is applied to all major assets to minimise losses from inefficient running of plant and machinery.	Through-life plans exist for all capital assets, covering spares, maintenance policy and end-of-life recovery.
M6.2 Process waste reduction	All manufacturing facilities produce data on product yields and waste streams - both value and physical quantities.	There is extensive team training in process control and waste elimination techniques.	Manufacturing facilities are viewed by local communities and other stakeholders as having minimal environmental impacts and positive social impacts.
M6.3 Data, measurement and incentives	The asset register holds full environmental data on all assets procured since the environmental policy was introduced. Energy and waste data is available and compared between sites.	Energy and waste reduction targets exist and are monitored by senior managers.	Waste and energy reduction is an integral part of continual improvement activities (including relevant incentives).

Plan

- S&OP
- Run strategy design
- Finished goods inventory management
- Finished goods replenishment planning
- Strategic supply planning
- Tactical supply planning
- Materials inventory management
- Materials replenishment management
- New product introduction
- Sustainability in planning

4 Plan

Really effective organisations have robust and well integrated planning processes controlling all functional activity.

Planning is central to supply chain management and establishes the parameters and control techniques within which the supply chain operates. In this way, the supply chain becomes aligned with product and service offerings, and overall company strategy.

Critically, these sc**prime**® sections should be used to assess how well the planning processes work together to manage the end-to-end supply chain organisation, and how planning processes are aligned with overall business needs.

End-to-end planning takes, as the input, the required demand, and configures resources to ensure efficient and robust supply in the short, medium and long term.

Sales and Operations Planning (S&OP) is a longer term process, ensuring there is capacity available so that supply meets demand requirements up to five years out, and that operational and financial plans are aligned. A structured S&OP process is recognised as a critical element in planning the supply chain, providing long term visibility of end-to-end supply chain plans over time, enabling better and clearer decision making, and aligning the supply chain with business objectives. It is the 'glue' that holds the operation together.

Run strategy design achieves the optimal balance between supply costs, inventory costs and service requirements through setting batch sizes and supply cycles. This process, as part of the overall supply chain strategy, is an integral part of planning and balancing demand against supply to optimise costs and service levels.

New Product Introduction (NPI) ensures smooth and effective phase-in and out of products by coordinating processes such as materials planning and supply management. The successful introduction of new products can be a lifeline for some companies, particularly if they operate in dynamic marketplaces. Depending on the business strategy, leading, matching or closely following trends by the successful launching of new products is often a key part of business operations.

Finished goods inventory management defines inventory targets, based on required service levels (safety stock) and balancing against production changeovers (cycle stock). It also allows inventory to be managed to ensure stock accuracy and stock rotation.

Finished goods replenishment planning defines a plan for meeting demand through deploying inventory in the network, and ensures that appropriate control techniques are used to drive efficiency and robustness. Strategic and tactical supply planning optimises the supply plan, typically assigning SKU production to factories to achieve the lowest total delivered cost whilst meeting customer service targets. Together, these processes configure the resources that ensure efficient supply.

Materials inventory management and materials replenishment management cover the management of material inventory and supply, including inventory level setting and control, obsolescence, delivery management and supplier quality assurance. The objective is to deliver the required service levels of material supply, balancing the cost of working capital, and also to ensure that all stock records and controls are in place.

Finally, sustainability in planning recognises that the efficiency and effectiveness of the planning process impacts the efficiency and environmental footprint of all other supply chain activities.

P1 Sales and operations planning

The Sales and Operations Planning process (S&OP) synchronises operating plans with demand requirements, tracks performance against budget and agrees gap-closing actions.

Description
This profile applies to all locations that are planning and balancing supply and demand either locally, regional or globally. The overall S&OP process should be viewed as a tightly integrated set of process steps.

Context
A structured S&OP process is recognised as a critical element in planning the supply chain, providing long term visibility of end-to-end supply chain plans over time, enabling better and clearer decision making.

Glossary
NPD

Abbreviation for New Product Development, the process by which new products or services are developed by the organisation for its customers.

P1 Sales and operations planning

P1 Elements	Competency	Proficiency	Mastery
P1.1 Policy	The Sales and Operations Planning (S&OP) process is documented, with defined scope, participants, inputs and outputs for each stage.	The S&OP process documentation is regularly updated. The S&OP process documentation is easily accessible. The S&OP process defines the outline agenda, inputs and outputs for each meeting.	The S&OP process is reviewed at least annually and is improved and updated according to requirements. The S&OP team members review process effectiveness after each cycle. The S&OP policy includes expected decision making rights (what/who/how) by step and overall.
P1.2 Process	Meeting dates are circulated at least 4 months in advance. Standardised document formats are used throughout the process. The process integrates Demand Management and Supply Management. Any New Product Introduction (NPI) is managed as part of the S&OP process. Supporting materials (pre-reads and agenda) are issued at least 24 hours in advance of each meeting.	The monthly cycle consists of pre-planned meetings, with each process step using a short meeting to review and approve recommendations. The outputs of the S&OP process define the single recognised operating plan for the organisation. Volume and financial data is reconciled bottom-up and top-down. The S&OP process is the key decision making forum for the business, and the decisions it makes are adopted and actioned throughout the organisation.	The S&OP process produces the majority of the required information for the annual budgeting process. Monthly gaps versus strategy and budget are analysed, with closing actions driving improvement prioritisation. Key decisions are supported by appropriate analysis and business cases of alternative scenarios including sensitivity analysis. All assumptions and business cases are documented.

P1.3 Planning horizon	Meetings focus on significant changes from the previous month and deviations from previously agreed plans.	Long-term planning is by brand/family for at least the next 12 months. Short-term planning (3-6 months) is pro-rated to SKU level. The planning horizon extends to the current financial year and at least 6 months of the next financial year.	Long-term planning is by brand/family for next 18 months. The S&OP process aligns operational decision making with the longer term (2-5 year) strategic business plan.
P1.4 Involvement	The S&OP meetings are attended by Sales, Production and Logistics/Distribution, with participants and roles clearly defined. Final approval meetings are chaired by a senior stakeholder of the S&OP cycle. Attendees are able to make the majority of decisions with only key strategic issues being escalated outside of the meeting.	The S&OP meetings are also attended appropriately by Engineering, Procurement and Marketing, with participants and roles clearly defined. Alternate attendees are agreed in advance if participants are not available. The role of Finance in the meeting cycle is clearly defined.	Meeting attendees are able to agree mitigating actions if previously agreed actions are not achieved. There is a documented list of alternates who represent their function when the normal attendee cannot be present. Meetings are attended by representatives with full decision-making responsibility.
P1.5 Integration with forecasts	Monthly forecasts revise anticipated results, reviewed during the S&OP review. The demand planning and management processes are fully integrated with the forecasting process, ensuring that the forecast accurately reflects all sales and marketing activities, including new product launches and product phase-outs.	There is a single set of demand and financial forecasts which are aligned with the demand/sales plan. Any variations/shortfalls against financial or volume targets are noted and discussed as part of the process. Monthly forecast identifies specific actions to improve anticipated results. The assumptions upon which the demand plan is based are monitored, reviewed and updated at least monthly.	The monthly forecast identifies specific actions to improve anticipated results. Forecast assumptions are reviewed on an on-going basis. The demand plan is used to develop financial projections of sales revenues, cash flow, and profit margins and the effect on budgets is calculated and reported monthly.

(continued on next page)

P1 Elements

P1.6 Integration with operational planning

Competency	Proficiency	Mastery
The S&OP process provides the escalation point for significant demand/supply imbalances. Key decisions resulting from the S&OP cycle are reflected in the day-to-day operational planning. Key decisions resulting from the S&OP cycle are reflected in the New Product Development (NPD) pipeline.	All operational planning processes are integrated with S&OP, with formal inputs and outputs to the S&OP steps. A review of tactical planning (1-6 months horizon) performance is included in the supply management step, with a focus on the longer term improvement agenda rather than short term issues. There is a clear process for communicating decisions back into the operational planning processes. The S&OP process sets the customer priorities for constrained supply and approves any updates to supply parameters such as inventory coverage or cycle times.	The strategic and tactical supply planning processes operate on the same assumptions which are validated by S&OP. Upsides and risks to the demand plan are well communicated and managed through to the operation processes where required, especially for new products. The S&OP process is a 2-way, taking a snapshot of the operational plans once a month to aid decision making and financial projections whilst ensuring the supply chain is best configured to meet the latest demand forecast.

Plan

P2 Run strategy design

This process achieves the optimal balance between supply costs, inventory costs and service requirements through setting batch sizes and supply cycles.

Description

This process, as part of the overall supply chain strategy, is an integral part of planning and balancing demand against supply to optimise costs and service levels.

Context

This process sets the overall strategy within which supply planning can take place. It is closely associated with Inventory management processes, since batch sizes and re-visit frequencies are directly related to cycle stock levels. The process should also be carried out within the guidelines of the S&OP process and sets the horizons to which the supply planning processes operate.

Glossary

MOQs

Abbreviation for Minimum Order Quantities.

P2 Elements	Competency	Proficiency	Mastery
P2.1 Product to plant allocations	Planning operates to a single customer service proposition. The cost to produce is calculated using a standard manufacturing overhead allocation, line efficiency rates and average changeover costs. Products are assigned to lines based upon available capacity.	Planning operates to various service propositions aligned to specific product and/or customer groups. The cost to produce is calculated using product based efficiency rates and associated changeover costs. Products are assigned to lines based upon the cost to produce and serve from each viable location, and is revisited on an adhoc basis.	Planning understands the customer service propositions past its own customer and aims to optimise the supply chain up to that point. The cost to produce is calculated using full activity based costing for all direct and indirect manufacturing and material input costs. All product to line allocations are reviewed collectively on a quarterly basis, to minimise the total cost to produce and serve.
P2.2 Production re-visit frequencies (cycles)	Production revisit frequencies are based on simple guidelines of product volumes, defined by product categories. The Minimum Order Quantites (MOQs) are based on optimising production efficiencies.	Revisit frequencies are calculated by balancing production costs with inventory costs, and repeated annually for all products. The MOQs are set so as not to impact running performance.	Revisit frequencies are calculated by optimising production, distribution and inventory costs across the length of the supply chain that can be influenced by the planners.
P2.3 Planning horizons	There is a common understanding of the planning horizons being used by the planning teams, including frozen, firm, slushy and liquid horizons. There is designated functional ownership for each planning zone.	Targets are in place to reduce the length of the frozen, firm and slushy windows.	Targets are in place to reduce the planning buckets within each of the frozen, firm and slushy windows.

Plan

P3 Finished goods inventory management

Inventory management is the process by which optimal target inventory levels of finished goods throughout the supply chain are defined, and inventory is managed to ensure stock accuracy and correct stock rotation.

Description

This profile covers inventory management of finished goods only. The objective is to deliver the required service levels whilst balancing the cost of working capital. This is done by setting inventory policy and parameters to balance demand and supply, taking account of demand and supply variation, production lead-times, batch sizes, changeover costs and capacity as well as manufacturing and working capital costs. In addition stock records must be kept accurate and up to date, and stock rotation managed to minimise obsolescence.

Context

Inventory management is a critical function in determining the trade-off of working capital levels against product availability and customer service levels. There is a strong relationship with the Production run strategy, which defines manufacturing batch sizes, and with Network design and management which sets the number of manufacturing and stockholding points.

Inventory management is the process by which optimal target inventory levels of finished goods throughout the supply chain are defined, and inventory is managed to ensure stock accuracy and correct stock rotation.

Glossary

Cycle counting

Process by which stock levels are continually monitored removing the need for a periodic total stock take (subject to the business's financial controls). Each stock item has its own frequency of count and accuracy tolerance depending on criticality and value.

SLOBs

Abbreviation for Slow Moving and Obsolete Stock.

P3 Finished goods inventory management

P3 Elements	Competency	Proficiency	Mastery
P3.1 Policy	There is a documented procedure for stock level setting, and documented stock targets for all stock points. The review frequency, tools and required communication for setting stock levels are documented.	The responsibility for achieving stock targets is clearly communicated and included in personal objectives. The procedure is applied consistently across all major inventory holding locations.	Stock targets are documented for all stock points by product category. The procedure is applied consistently across all inventory holding locations.
P3.2 Inventory setting	There are high-level guidelines for defining stock levels. Stock targets are reviewed annually or more often if there are particular circumstances which change.	Inventory policies differ per product category, such as slow movers, which may be held in fewer locations. Stock targets are reviewed at least every six months. Safety stock levels are calculated scientifically based on demand variability.	Inventory is balanced through stock transfers as well as replenishment. Safety stock levels are calculated at least quarterly, based on demand and supply variability to achieve the required service levels at minimum total supply chain cost. Safety stock levels are calculated scientifically based on the more accurate of demand variability and forecast error. The demand plan is based on a statistically generated baseline if the safety stock is based on the demand variability.

(continued on next page)

P3 Finished goods inventory management

P3 Elements	Competency	Proficiency	Mastery
P3.3 Stock accuracy	Stock accuracy is measured at location level. There are regular stock checks at key financial points (e.g. quarterly). Inventory errors are corrected as they are uncovered.	Cycle counting frequencies have been established with defined accuracy tolerances. The frequency of inventory usage and/or value drives stock check frequency and accuracy targets. A process to eliminate causes of errors is in place.	Perpetual inventory counting procedures are in place. Cycle stock counting has replaced the process of annual stock takes. Inventory accuracy is reviewed at least monthly, with root cause analysis and actions to improve accuracy.
P3.4 Visibility and integration	Almost all inventory points are included in the regional inventory planning process. There is full visibility of all inventories across divisions/regions.	There is a process in place to ensure end-to-end inventory optimisation occurs throughout the regional/global network. For all 'handovers' of inventory between business units, there is a process in place to ensure there are not multiple buffers of safety stock.	The regional/global inventory planning process has full control over all supply and inventory points. There is visibility of customer inventories and supplier finished goods inventories. The differing costs of inventory at each level of the network are fully understood.
P3.5 Inventory requirements planning	The demand plan is spread equally across the month to give an opening stock requirement for each week. There are no demand forecast consumption rules from week to week, but the total for the month remains unaltered.	The demand plan is phased across the month using a profile that best reflects the historic and/or future distribution by week. Forecast consumption rules operate within the month, and can roll unconsumed demand into the next week and/or rest of the month.	The demand plan is distributed into daily buckets that can be dynamically reallocated within the week, month or wider. Forecast consumption rules can roll unconsumed demand into the next month.

P3.6 Stock obsolescence

The value of slow moving stocks has been quantified and improvement targets have been set. There is a designated business owner for Slow Moving or Obsolete Stock (SLOBs) reporting and movement. Products with shelf-life issues are managed effectively to highlight expiring stocks for immediate usage or quarantining. Strict quarantining/destruction procedures are in place.	Actions to reduce the volume and value of slow-moving stocks are identified in the monthly Sales and Operations Planning (S&OP) process. Finance understand why SLOBs are generated and allow for sufficient inventory write-offs each year. Shelf-life criteria is built into stock ordering and stock usage/rotation routines.	Root causes of SLOBs are assessed and the lessons learnt are used to improve inventory management. SLOBs generated rates are tracked and reported to S&OP.

P4 Finished goods replenishment planning

Replenishment planning defines a despatch and inventory plan for each stockholding point and demand location.

Description

This is based on actual and forecast demand, and is carried out through calculating appropriate replenishment quantities and timings that ensure customer service and optimise production logistics costs. This profile covers replenishment planning of finished goods only. The objective is to develop a practical and cost effective plan for achieving required service levels.

Context

In some cases, demand is in the form of firm orders, defining quantities and due dates. Another model is VMI (Vendor Managed Inventory), where the supplier can plan replenishments to achieve agreed stock or availability targets (for internal or external 'customers'). Replenishment planning is focused on VMI demand, and is also critical in multi-tiered distribution chains when stock of the same SKU is held at more than one location across the supply chain. The distribution requirements plan feeds directly into master production scheduling.

Glossary

VMI

Abbreviation for Vendor Managed Inventory - a process whereby the supplier ensures the availability of products to the customer by controlling the levels of stock.

P4 Finished goods replenishment planning

P4 Elements	Competency	Proficiency	Mastery
P4.1 Replenishment and control techniques	A documented replenishment model is in place which defines the responsibilities of each business unit and function.	There is more than one documented replenishment model in place as appropriate to different customers and needs. There is at least a 12 month view of planned replenishments for each demand point.	There is a drive towards greater adoption of Vendor Managed Inventory (VMI), with specific plans in place for significant volumes. The replenishment horizon looks beyond 12 months as an input to the supply management process.
P4.2 Replenishment calculations	The replenishment calculation focuses on achieving the required service levels and inventory targets. The replenishment calculation takes into account any key constraints in the distribution network, such as shipping calendars and vessel sizes. Lead-times are as stated by the logistics provider.	The warehouse, transport and inventory cost implications of the replenishment plan are calculated and understood. Lead-times are as demonstrated in the previous 12 months.	The replenishment plan optimises total costs while achieving the required service levels. A number of different options are considered before deciding on the optimal plan. There is an explicit objective to smooth distribution over the period available to reduce peaks in resource needs.

P4.3 Exception resolution	There are procedures to resolve exceptions such as when demand requirements cannot be met.	There are clear escalation paths for unresolved issues, depending on their criticality and risk. Time-to-respond metrics are a part of the escalation process. Customer requirements are well understood through regular communications.	Replenishment priority by brand and customer is clearly defined through the Sales and Operations Planning (S&OP) process. Regular communication with customers provides an up-to-date understanding of their costs and priorities. Decision making enables costs to be minimised (e.g. consolidating orders to enable full vehicle loads).
P4.4 Automation and scalability	Replenishment planning is supported by systems (or Excel).	Replenishment planning is automated, using appropriate software to provide scalability and robustness.	Replenishment planning software is integrated to other planning systems, including key logistics providers.

Strategic supply planning configures and conditions the supply chain to meet future demand through cost effective use of resources.

Description
Strategic supply planning ensures all required resources (materials, manufacturing and warehousing/ distribution) are available to meet the demand plan whilst being used in a cost effective manner. It assigns demand to factories, and is generally a monthly process.

Context
This profile applies to all locations which are involved in planning supply to meet demand and should be viewed as part of a set of tightly integrated process steps within the overall S&OP process. It assigns demand to factories, and makes decisions on changing capacities to fit demand.

Glossary
Rough Cut Capacity Planning

Abbreviated to RCCP. This process uses simplified capacity constraints to check the feasibility of the supply and demand plan. The process also recommends any actions required to make the plan feasible.

P5 Elements	Competency	Proficiency	Mastery
P5.1 Approach	The strategic supply planning process is integrated with Sales and Operations Planning (S&OP) cycle and reviewed monthly. Supply analysis is based upon critical resource requirements by product family, expected volumes, historic mix and inventory. Aggregate stock levels are identified to achieve the desired service levels, and projected across the entire planning horizon. Constrained supply planning is conducted for main production stage only.	The supply management process primarily focuses on cost effectively achieving desired service levels with minimal inventory. Supply planning can be viewed and constrained by a number of key resources. Assumptions and/or vulnerabilities for production and sourcing are documented on a monthly basis. Constrained supply planning is conducted for all Production stages and Logistics. The capacity plan is based on an understanding of market growth values and investment lead-times.	Alternative supply plans are developed for each demand scenario. Supply planning is constrained by all key resources. Supplier capability and long lead-time materials are treated as critical resources. Constrained supply planning is conducted for all operational stages in the company's supply chain. The capacity plan is reviewed and agreed by the operations board.

(continued on next page)

P5 Elements	Competency	Proficiency	Mastery
P5.2 Capacity planning	The capacity plan is built bottom up with all maintenance requirements, improvement plans and new product start-up curves included. There is a clear view of overall capacity against demand. Exceptions, such as lack of capacity, are managed in the short term (2–3 months), with such variables as stock builds or adding shifts.	There is a clear view of capacity over the 12-18 month horizon and key growth lines are reviewed as part of the supply review. Decisions are made on mid-term capacity where required (e.g. stock builds, up-staffing or incremental investment). Planning rates reflect potential output enhancements and product mix changes. The Rough Cut Capacity Planning (RCCP) process is carried out for the next 18 months on all critical resources.	Low, middle and upside volume scenarios are used to test capacity. For each product group, the decision between using excess capacity or safety stock is based upon the optimal cost/service trade-off. Over the longer term (12 months +) horizon, the process is used to recommend asset investment strategies across all product lines. Capacity strategy provides a key input into strategic business planning. The impact of alternative supply plans on constraining resources is quantified and required actions are clearly identified.
P5.3 Capacity constraints techniques	Total actual versus planned production is reported monthly by product family. Volume gaps between actual and planned production are investigated each month.	The validity of data and assumptions is reviewed every month for the agreed plan and budget. Major changes to capacity are supported by documented assumptions.	Changes to capacity elements are monitored for the first few cycles to ensure validity. Actual year-to-date capacity is checked versus budgeted capacity to highlight potential shortfalls. Potential shortfalls in capacity are addressed and the revised projected capacity is communicated.

P5.4 Systems

A capacity planning tool (or Excel) is used to support capacity planning.	Capacity and demand planning systems are integrated. Capacity and demand planning modules are utilised by 'expert users'.	The capacity and demand planning modules are integrated within the business enterprise system. Users are fully trained to use the functionality appropriate for their area. The risks and benefits of deploying additional software functionality are regularly assessed.

Plan

P6 Tactical supply planning

This process creates the supply plan, typically assigning SKU production to factories in weekly buckets, to achieve lowest total delivered cost whilst meeting customer service targets.

Description

Working within the constraints of the strategic supply plan, the tactical supply plan provides a statement of planned future production and sets the timings and quantities of individual production runs.

Context

Creating a tactical supply plan that in total agrees with the strategic supply plan (within agreed tolerances) is a key step in making sure the material and capacity plans are not mis-stated and the anticipated results as defined by the S&OP plan are met.

Glossary

Rough Cut Capacity Planning

Abbreviated to RCCP. This planning uses simplified capacity constraints to check the feasibility of the supply and demand plan. The process also recommends any actions required to make the plan feasible.

Rough Cut Materials Plan
Abbreviated to RCMP. The intent of rough cut materials planning is to convert supply plans into the impact on critical materials needed to carry out those plans.

P6 Elements	Competency	Proficiency	Mastery
P6.1 Approach	Tactical planning translates the demand into time phased weekly supply plans for production, materials and logistics. The plan covers resources and material supply, and reviews focus only on exceptions.	The Run Strategy rules are used to generate an achievable plan for the following 3 months. Processes for Rough Cut Capacity Planning (RCCP) and Rough Cut Materials Planning (RCMP) are used to test plan for availability of major resource groups and materials. There is limited off-line assessment of 2-3 alternative solutions before a final schedule is created.	The Run Strategy rules are used to generate an achievable plan over the entire planning horizon. On-line 'what-if' modelling is used to assess alternative solutions. Alternative plans are costed and presented as part of the supply management meeting. Rough cut sequencing is applied over a thee month horizon outside of the firm plan. Differing planning horizons are recognised for Lean and Agile product streams (Lean has longer fixed planning horizon versus that of Agile).
P6.2 Integration	There is a meeting attended by Production and Materials Management to review and agree the tactical plan. The tactical plan is reviewed and updated monthly.	The tactical planning process includes input from Logistics and Materials Planning. The tactical plan is reviewed and updated weekly. The tactical plan is governed by the Sales and Operations Planning (S&OP) cycle and key decisions approved as part of a monthly supply review step.	The tactical planning process is integrated with Customer Service reviews to reflect latest performance levels and key demand changes.

(continued on next page)

P6.3 Execution	The tactical plan is in at least a weekly bucket level of granularity. The plan is suggested by the 'master scheduler' based on capacity analysis, consideration of material availability and manually refined locally with logistics.	Some violation of released production plans occurs but only as part of a defined abnormal events process. Finite capacity planning is used to optimise the production plans in the short-term horizon.	Planning is a continual process with the tactical plan element in daily buckets.
P6.4 Plan stability	The tactical planning process does not impact the SKUs planned within the short term frozen horizon. Within an agreed firm planning horizon, production quantities maybe changed subject to production and material capacity analysis but the SKUs remain constant unless absolutely critical.	The plan stability within the agreed firm planning horizon is measured and reported. Make-to-Order items are pinned to a fixed week to reflect required lead times, whereas Make-to-Stock quantities can flex providing the inventory min/max targets are not violated.	Any major proposed SKU changes are communicated to key suppliers to test material availability prior to plan being formally amended.

This profile covers the management of raw material inventory level setting and control.

Description

The objective is to deliver the required material service level, balancing the cost of working capital, and also to ensure that all stock records and controls are in place.

Context

Ineffective materials management will lead to service issues, over-stocking and obsolescence, resulting in lost revenue or excessive working capital.

Glossary

VMI

Abbreviation for Vendor Managed Inventory - a process whereby the supplier ensures the availability of products to the customer by controlling the levels of stock.

SLA

Abbreviation for a Service Level Agreement, an agreement between the supplying and receiving parties defining how the service is provided. At its most basic, an SLA details service and quality levels, but can cover every aspect of supply from cost, delivery, returns, innovation and improvement. The SLA usually forms a part of the contract between the two parties.

Cycle counting

Process by which stock levels are continually monitored removing the need for a periodic total stock take (subject to the business's financial controls). Each stock item has its own frequency of count and accuracy tolerance depending on criticality and value.

P7 Materials inventory management

P7 Elements	Competency	Proficiency	Mastery
P7.1 Stock management	Inventory plans with consistent approaches and targets are in place. Targets are applied to stock at internal locations. The supplier's lead-time is held on the customer's system for regularly bought items. A program is in place to reduce variety of similar items through consolidation.	Inventory plans define key principles, KPIs and service levels. Stock is held by both the customer and the supplier with targets set and levels measured. Stock information is available to each party upon request. Product lead-times, min/max levels etc. are deployed on customer's item master system records. Physical site storage plans are in place to optimise access and scope for expansion/contraction based on business needs.	Inventory plans are agreed and co-developed with tier 1 suppliers using their knowledge of lower tiers. Stock available in the supply chain is viewed and measured as total stock regardless of whether it is at an internal location or with the supplier. The balance of 'what is held where' is governed by physical logistics of supply. There is a proactive and collaborative approach to supply, optimising response time and cost of stock. The supplier holds stock at the last build point before specific customer configuration. There is active management of site space to match business needs with a focus on easy access in/out, safety, warehousing and inventory systems and total costs (fixed & variable). Costs are transparent and jointly reviewed and managed.

P7.2 Inventory setting	There is a good understanding of the safety and cycle stock elements of inventory holdings and the detailed drivers of each. Stock-outs prompt a review of related parameters. Stock levels are set scientifically.	Parameters to set stock levels for required delivery performance are well understood and regularly reviewed within the organisation. Stock targets are reviewed at least every six months, or more often if there are particular circumstances which change. Key suppliers work collaboratively to challenge parameters and minimise stock levels. A Vendor Managed Inventory (VMI) approach is defined and implemented with key suppliers. Consignment stocking is considered for key components with buy-back agreements.	In appropriate situations, joint customer/supplier planning is undertaken to optimise service but minimise overall inventory holding costs, often via KPI and other metrics visible via internet portal-type mechanisms. There is a documented procedure which is adhered to for stock level setting, specifying frequency, techniques and communication. Inventory levels are recalculated at least quarterly based on changing volumes, demand variability, supplier capabilities etc. For consignment stocking or VMI arrangements, all changes in planned inventory levels are documented in Service Level Agreements (SLAs). There is an ongoing process to challenge the need for stock, particularly consumables.
B7.3 Stock accuracy	Stock accuracy is measured at location level. Regular stock checks (e.g. quarterly) occur at key financial points. Errors are corrected as they are uncovered. Perpetual inventory counting procedures are in place for all materials.	Stock is accurate at location level. Frequency and accuracy targets relate to frequency of usage and/or value. A process to eliminate causes of errors is in place. Key suppliers have similar processes to validate stock levels.	There is regular (at least monthly) review of inventory accuracy, with root cause analysis and actions to improve accuracy. Cycle counting is fully operational, driving error prevention groups with no annual stock takes required. Appropriate usage of optimisation software ensures cost/service trade-off is actively managed. Key suppliers operate similar advanced stock management processes. Responsibility for maintaining and improving processes and accuracy lies with a dedicated materials management resource.

(continued on next page)

P7 Elements

P7.4 Stock rotation

Competency	Proficiency	Mastery
Material stocks are rotated on a strict First In, First Out (FIFO) basis. Materials with shelf-life issues are managed effectively to highlight expiring stocks for immediate usage or quarantining. Strict quarantining/destruction procedures are in place.	The value of slow moving stocks is quantified and improvement targets are set. Material shelf-life criteria is built into stock ordering and stock usage/rotation routines.	Reduction actions for slow moving stocks are identified as part of the monthly Sales and Operations Planning (S&OP) process.

Plan

P8 Materials replenishment management

This profile covers the management of raw material supply, including delivery management and supplier quality assurance.

Description

The objective is to deliver the required service levels of material supply.

Context

Ineffective material deployment will lead to service issues, over-stocking and obsolescence, resulting in lost revenue or excessive working capital. Materials management is carried out within the context of supplier contracts and internal manufacturing and warehousing constraints.

Glossary

MRP

Abbreviation for Materials Requirement Plan; this is a time-phased plan of materials requirements, generated through analysing the production plan and applying the BOM (bill-of-materials) for each item or SKU (stock-keeping unit). When the current stock levels, required safety stock levels, minimum order quantities and order lead times of each material item is taken into account, the optimal time to order each item is calculated.

P8 Materials replenishment management

This profile covers the management of raw material supply, including delivery management and supplier quality assurance.

VMI

Abbreviation for Vendor Managed Inventory - a process whereby the supplier ensures the availability of products to the customer by controlling the levels of stock.

Kanban

The method of replenishment of product of material where the signal for replenishment is based upon actual usage (versus predicted usage) i.e. the downstream customer 'pulls' the product/material when required, in the quantity required.

SLA

Abbreviation for a Service Level Agreement, an agreement between the supplying and receiving parties defining how the service is provided. At its most basic, an SLA details service and quality levels, but can cover every aspect of supply from cost, delivery, returns, innovation and improvement. The SLA usually forms a part of the contract between the two parties.

BOMs
Abbreviation for Bill of Materials.

OTIF
Abbreviation for deliveries being ‘On Time In Full’. This is a common metric in measuring the delivery element of a supplier’s performance.

P8 Materials replenishment management

P8 Elements	Competency	Proficiency	Mastery
P8.1 Control techniques	A Material Requirements Planning (MRP) process is used to achieve acceptable material availability, inventory levels and cost. Consensus forecast requirements are shared with suppliers. Call-offs are made from a pre-agreed contract against customer order and forecast.	A variety of control techniques are applied to achieve acceptable material availability, inventory levels and cost at a material item level. Control techniques drive the call-off mechanisms: firm period of schedule, Vendor Managed Inventory (VMI) or Kanban. Supplier schedules are used to communicate demand requirements over a longer term horizon.	Synchronised 'pull' control techniques are used as an appropriate method to minimise costs and lead time throughout the supply chain. Delivery frequencies and quantities are based on the total cost of ownership. Control techniques are reviewed regularly to reflect changes in demand patterns. Appropriate software is deployed to minimise transaction costs and complexity.
P8.2 MRP exception management	The MRP process is run at least weekly. Exceptions are identified and are resolved through changes to the production schedule where possible.	The MRP process is run as frequently as appropriate for the type of business, based on the latest production plan for each applicable site. Unless any exceptions are reported it is accepted that there are no materials issues with the current production plan. Where exceptions occur there are clear guidelines on their resolution depending on the cost effect and risk to customer service.	The MRP process is run on a daily net change basis to keep the material plan synchronised with the detailed manufacturing schedules. The number of exceptions is monitored and analysed using pareto analysis and criticality of the item (ABC products); the highest variances receive the most focus. Exception messages are prioritised by pre-agreed message type rules. All material orders respect agreed supplier lead times, unless there is an explicit exception agreed.

P8.3 Supplier schedules	Supplier schedules are updated and issued weekly or as appropriate for business needs. There is a frozen time period within the schedule where demand cannot be amended without consent of the supplier. There is an agreed feedback process for suppliers to input to the schedule.	There are time periods within the schedule horizon where the supplier is given commitment to manufacture and deliver. These commitment criteria are defined within the Service Level Agreement (SLA). Material call-off processes allow for less than a week's coverage to be achieved where required. Schedules give at least 12 week's visibility of forecasted demand. There are differentiated processes for critical items to ensure supply is maintained.	Different time periods within the schedule are agreed as commitments to the supplier - purchase material, make base/blanks, make final item etc. Commitment criteria are continually challenged by both parties to drive increasing flexibility. Material call-off processes allow for the lowest realistic number of days cover that the production environment can support. The supplier has appropriate access to the planning system.
P8.4 MRP parameters	There is defined ownership within the organisation for MRP parameters. The MRP parameters reflect relevant service levels. There is a documented process in place to monitor and update MRP parameters. Material usage and scrap factors in the planning Bill-Of-Materials (BOMs) are set as site averages.	The MRP parameters are reviewed at least quarterly. Lead times are specific to suppliers and include use of safety times where there is variability in lead times. Material utilisation discrepancies trigger a process capability and/or material quality review. Material usage and scrap factors in the planning BOMs are set as line averages.	All MRP parameters are accurate, with a defined process to measure and track accuracy. Lead times are a realistic reflection of each supplier's process time, plus physical transport time, plus acceptance time. Material usage and scrap factors in the planning BOMs are set as demonstrated product averages by line.
P8.5 Supplier delivery management	Selected suppliers have fixed nominated delivery windows (e.g. day and time +/- 2 hours). The On Time In Full (OTIF) delivery performance is measured for all suppliers.	A process exists for the originator to formally receive services. All suppliers have fixed nominated delivery windows. Supplier OTIF performance is tracked and root cause analysis is carried out (supplier and buyer) where targets are not met. Actions are then implemented to drive improvement. Supplier compliance on paperwork standards and packaging requirements (e.g. standard containers) is measured.	Receipts are automated via bar coding, there is a standard format with all suppliers. The supplier transmits delivery documentation in advance (e.g. Advanced Shipping Notices, certificates of conformity) by Electronic Data Interchanges or internet portal. Line-side supply is used for all appropriate goods/services.

Plan

P9 New product introduction

The New Product Introduction (NPI) process ensures full product availability at the time of product launch and minimises inventory and waste.

Description

This profile covers the key processes to manage supply of new products for market launch. It does not cover innovation/design.

Context

The successful introduction of new products is a critical process for many companies, particularly if they operate in dynamic marketplaces. Depending on the business strategy, leading, matching or closely following trends by the successful launch of new products is often a key part of business operations. Equally, failing to meet the timescales, costs or quality of new products can impact on business profile with customers and can damage profitability and lead to a loss in market share or penetration.

Glossary

MRP

Abbreviation for Materials Requirement Plan; this is a time-phased plan of materials requirements, generated through analysing the production plan and applying the BOM (bill of material) for each item or SKU (stock-keeping unit). When the current stock levels, required safety stock levels, minimum order quantities and order lead times of each material item is taken into account, the optimal time to order each item is calculated.

P9 New product introduction

P9 Elements	Competency	Proficiency	Mastery
P9.1 Policy and procedures	Formal New Product Introduction (NPI) procedures are in place and followed. The current NPI procedures recognise agreed time fences and lead-times.	The NPI procedures are reviewed regularly. The NPI procedures include task planning and control against agreed timescales.	The NPI procedures are continuously reviewed and improved. The NPI process is visible and understood by all involved and performance is reported.
P9.2 Launch planning	Suppliers are informed proactively of materials requirements. The NPI cycles are coordinated with the promotional calendar. New product planning is reviewed as part of the Sales and Operations Planning (S&OP) process.	Standard planning times are adhered to and performance is measured. The market up-take of new products is managed to match available volumes. One business function has sole responsibility for the management of the NPI process.	Accountability at each stage of the NPI process is clearly communicated. The NPI process is driven by goal-directed project management and parallel/ concurrent activity management. The NPI launches involve collaborative processes with supply chain partners (e.g. material suppliers and finished goods distributors) to improve time-to-market.
P9.3 Integration	There is an integrated approach between new product development and production. Cross-functional teams are nominated for product launch projects but not used consistently. Suppliers are involved for critical components.	New product launches are delivered by a cross-functional team working across related business processes. Key suppliers are involved in design, planning and execution from new product concept through to launch. Product design takes into account the full lifecycle of the product.	New product introduction is managed as a cross functional activity with fully concurrent design of product and process. Major suppliers are fully integrated into entire NPI process and are seen to add value to the success of a launch.

P9.4 Execution	All internal functions are involved in new product introduction execution. At least half of launches are implemented within timescales and within cost/resource plans. Key elements of over-run NPI projects are recognised and built into revised process steps.	The post-launch review is a key part of the process and lessons are proactively communicated and built into all related processes. All internal functions are involved in planning new product introduction. Potential over-runs/delays of new product launches are identified early enough to allow for corrective action.	Post-launch reviews drive continual improvement of product launches.
P9.5 Systems	Standard project management systems are used.	The product launch is supported by integrated systems of forecasting and planning.	Integrated planning and execution systems are deployed to support the NPI process.
P9.6 Inventory planning	There is a detailed planning process in place for new products, ensuring sufficient quantities for launch.	The NPI inventory planning process is based on minimising waste of the old product. Inventory targets for new products are based upon a launch profile for similar products in local or regional market. New product launch inventory levels are reviewed as part of the S&OP process. A plan exists to respond to market demands (either increased or decreased) following the initial product launch.	There is a detailed daily review of sales and production during the critical handover period to monitor availability. Contingencies exist where product may be unsold if a launch is unsuccessful.
P9.7 Material planning	Suppliers are kept informed of materials requirements for new products as soon as they appear in Material Requirements Planning (MRP).	Delivery schedules and warehousing space for large quantities for a product launch are planned in advance of formal MRP release.	There is close liaison with suppliers to rapidly flex production up or down in early stages to manage uncertainty and minimise potential obsolescence. A matrix containing the agreed lead times with each supplier for any new development is updated at least once a year.

Sustainability in planning ensures that materials and products are managed across the supply chain to minimise the environmental impact whilst maintaining service levels and financial metrics.

Description

Sustainability within planning applies to all activities which plan and schedule raw materials, production, storage, distribution and the sales of finished product. These activities can be at a local, regional or global level.

Context

Whilst much of the environmental impact of a product is locked in at the design and sourcing stage, planning decisions - at strategic, tactical and operational levels – can help minimise impact if carried out in an informed manner.

Glossary

VSA

Abbreviation for Value Stream Analysis. VSA is an integral part of 'Lean' thinking. It is a tool to look at a business process, defining value and non-value adding steps, identifying opportunities for eliminating non-value adding activities and areas of waste.

P10 Sustainability in planning

P10 Elements	Competency	Proficiency	Mastery
P10.1 Materials planning	Planning of all major material flows considers environmental impacts when deciding frequency of movement, volumes, distances and transport mode.	Inbound distribution networks are modelled at least annually to identify options to minimise environmental impacts.	Inbound distribution networks are modelled at least every 6 months to identify options to minimise environmental impacts. Distribution network models are shared with procurement and finished product planning teams to optimise global activities.
P10.2 Product and channel planning	A Value Stream Analysis (VSA) is conducted on some high volume product flows to identify impact of end-to-end supply chain activities.	Proposed changes to channel plans within the network are evaluated using a modular VSA approach.	Environmental impact assessments are updated annually for all channels and markets. Impact assessments drive improvement in effectiveness of planning activities at each stage of the supply chain.
P10.3 Range planning	Basic environmental impacts are considered when planning future range offerings and customer service levels.	Future range plans have high level targets set for reducing environmental impacts.	A board-level strategy is in place to seek competitive advantage based on continuously diminishing supply chain impacts.
P10.4 Data, measurement and incentives	Data exists on material, packaging and product flows to enable simple impact analysis to be carried out.	Metrics are in place to measure and predict the environmental impact of future planned activity against historical data.	Staff are incentivised to optimise material and product flows to deliver reduced supply chain impacts.

Deliver

Network design & management

Warehouse planning

Warehouse operations

Warehouse performance management

Transport operations

Transport performance management

Contractor management

Sustainability in delivery

5 Deliver

The Deliver function manages all product movements and storage for both inbound materials and outbound finished goods. Typically, total costs in these areas represent a high proportion of total supply chain costs and mistakes result in service failures, so efficiency and robustness are critical.

As products, services and customer needs change over time the distribution network must adapt as well. This may mean changes to the logistics infrastructure and how it is used. These changes may require significant capital investment, so must be judged correctly and planned. The performance of the whole network should be managed month by month through a review cycle based on meaningful metrics; this process triggers short term fixes as well as longer term structural changes. These aspects are covered in the network design and management section.

The use of third party logistics providers is increasingly becoming the norm in many industries, with the objective of reducing risk, cost and organisational complexity. The contractor management section describes how to best carry out the contracting process, and also how to manage contracts when they are in place.

Managing warehouses is a core capability in the Deliver function. Storage may be required for very different types of products, with different needs in terms of environment, security and handling. High efficiency and accuracy, and low costs, are driven by having the correct layout for the facility in the first instance, ensuring performance measures are in place to maximise both picking rates and accuracy and that the appropriate systems are in place to support the facility.

Suppliers may be spread globally. Customers vary in size and different routes to market are common; direct to businesses, via retail or distributors, and potentially direct to consumers. The planning of routes to cover inbound and outbound movements, and multiple customer deliveries, is an important part of ensuring service requirements are met at minimum cost. Products may have to be picked up from customers and returned. International product movements require correct and timely documentation. Overall performance must be tracked and managed. All of these factors make managing transport challenging, and are covered in the transport management section.

Deliver operations can have a significant effect on the environment. Many countries have stringent regulations, and many organisations have internal guidelines which require even higher standards. The sustainability in delivery section outlines the requirements to manage a sustainable logistics operation.

Deliver

D1 Network design and management

Network design and management includes strategic and tactical management of the end-to-end transport and warehousing functions, from manufacturing to end customer.

Description

The design aspect defines the location and function of stockholding and transit points, the major physical infrastructure therein, and the high level process flows that the business will operate. The key aspect of this role is to manage the trade-offs between transport and warehouse functions to ensure that the required level of end-customer service is achieved at the lowest cost with an acceptable level of risk.

Context

Transport and warehousing is a critical element of the supply chain, with a significant impact on costs and customer service. This profile measures how well the transport and warehousing network is planned and operated to meet business requirements. It is linked with the 'Warehouse management' and 'Transport management' profiles, as well as the 'Contractor management' profile where applicable. This profile applies to all operations that have distribution and stockholding operations and covers raw materials, WIP, finished goods and returns.

D1 Elements	Competency	Proficiency	Mastery
D1.1 Strategic design	The distribution network and supporting processes have been reviewed in the past three years, leading to changes in how the network has been used for specific product categories and destinations. Changes are made to product flow routing where necessary and each facility has a clear role in the network.	The network and operations design is the end product of a formal process, considering the balancing of cost and service levels. The design process has reviewed the number and type of warehouse locations (stocked warehouses and stockless transhipment points), transport types and routings. There is a clear plan in the network for how seasonal peaks will be handled. There is a formal, documented process which triggers a network review, based on elapsed time or changes in demand patterns. Product flow is reviewed on a periodic basis.	The network and operations design optimises end-to-end service and cost by considering supply source as well as customer location, both now and in the future and builds in flexibility to cope with future market structural changes. The design process considers: radical change, such as shared networks; moving some 'manufacturing' processes, like final product customisation, to warehouses; and, the appropriate routes to market for different products/customers, based on the delivery promise. All product flow routings are reviewed in real-time against pre-specified optimisation rules.

D1.2 Delivery promise	Customer demands are responded to as received, with no customer prioritisation. There is a single service level that applies to all customers.	The service level offered is based on being competitive in the market. Requests to deviate from the agreed service level are at the discretion of the operation. Clear rules exist as to how a product will be allocated in times of shortage, and a formal process exists if there is a requirement to deviate from this. There is a monthly review of performance by the customer between Sales and Supply Chain. Root cause analysis of issues and remedial action plans are followed through.	Delivery promise is used as key service input into network design. Groups of customers are prioritised, and a tiered service is offered to these groups on all aspects of the order to cash cycle. The delivery promise offered is based on being competitive in the market and from a cost to serve analysis. Depending on the priority given to the customer, non-compliance results in penalty charges with individual salesmen responsible for ensuring these penalties are paid. Internal failures charged against the budget of the 'offending' department. Where possible, the offerings are standardised (specifically around product presentation, minimum order quantities and lead times).
D1.3 Network performance	Transport and warehouse performance (cost and service) are reported at least monthly. There are operational reviews held at least monthly where performance measures and targets are reviewed, and the reviews create specific actions which are followed up until resolved.	Transport, warehouse and total logistics costs are tracked and reported weekly on a total distribution cost per unit basis. The RFP response includes pro formas (resources, productivity, cost) so that easy comparisons between competing bids can be made, and helps avoid contractor errors in data interpretation. Transport and warehouse service and productivity KPIs are clearly defined and reported monthly.	There is a weekly and monthly review cycle which aims to balance cost/service trade-off across its entire network. This process includes warehouse operational cost, transport operational cost, inventory holding and service levels across all relevant territories. Differences in performance between sites are analysed and used as the basis of process standardisation and continuous improvement. Risks and issues feed into strategic design processes. The KPIs are aligned through the network and supply chain, and the impact of failure elsewhere in the supply chain on network cost and service performance is reviewed and measured.

Warehouse planning ensures that warehouses are configured and resourced effectively to meet the demand requirements.

Description

This profile applies to all operations which directly control warehousing and covers warehousing of all raw materials, WIP and finished goods.

Context

Warehousing is a critical element of the supply chain, with a significant impact on quality, costs and customer service since it plays a role in feeding manufacturing with raw materials and supplying finished goods to customers as well as handling returns.

Glossary

Activity Based Costing (ABC)

An approach that attributes costs to activities, objects and processes to support accurate product and process costing.

D2 Elements	Competency	Proficiency	Mastery
D2.1 Configuration and capacity	The Manufacturing or Planning functions inform the warehouse of what seasonal stockholding is expected to be and warehouse storage capacity is an input to planning processes. There are logical flows through receipt, put-away, picking and despatch to minimise double handling and travel distances. The SKUs are allocated their own picking location, and laid out in a logical ABC order based on accessions. Returns are handled separately from good stock.	Warehouse storage and throughput capacity are built into the supply chain planning and resource management processes, with stock levels set statistically to take account of supply and demand variability. The warehouse layout has been reviewed in the past 12 months for product handling, storage and workflow design. There is clear product category demarcation (e.g. quarantined and free stock, returns and good stock). Clearance of dead/obsolete stock takes place at least twice a year.	Stock optimisation is regularly reviewed by SKU (ABC categories) taking into account the total business cost to serve. Capability for 'what-if' inventory optimisation and warehouse capacity modelling exists based on algorithms which deal with different demand patterns. The warehouse layout review optimised the stockholding, throughput and added-value functions of the warehouse and considered all feasible picking methodologies (given the existing racking infrastructure). Seasonal reviews of ABC product velocity (line item movement frequency) and product handling characteristics are undertaken and storage locations and flows are optimised. There are clear rules agreed with Sales for removing and writing off dead stock to release warehouse space.

(continued on next page)

D2 Elements	Competency	Proficiency	Mastery
D2.2 Plan distribution staffing requirements	The command and control structure enables all functions to operate efficiently and effectively. Resources are balanced between the various operations within the warehouse.	Standards are used to calculate resource needs. The weekly activity profile in each department through the week is known and staff are cross-trained so they can move from one task to another as needed. Tasks (e.g. intake, picking, loading) are scheduled throughout the day to minimise total staff numbers whilst satisfying required service levels. Peak/promotion/holiday times are planned and medium term resource planning is in place up to 6 months ahead.	Performance in peaks is carefully monitored to minimise overstaffing occurrences. Variations in daily/weekly/seasonal workflows are known and solutions planned to mitigate these (e.g. a flexible workforce with core shift and flexible shift patterns is used, or an annualised hours scheme). Long term resource planning includes having a 'pool' of trained seasonal workers who can be called on to minimise service issues.

Deliver

D3 Warehouse operations

Warehouse operations ensure that warehouses meet required levels of quality (on-time/in-full despatch as well as inventory holding accuracy) as cost effectively as possible.

Description

This profile applies to all operations which directly control warehousing and covers warehousing of all raw materials, WIP and finished goods.

Context

Warehousing is a critical element of the supply chain, with a significant impact on quality, costs and customer service since it plays a role in feeding manufacturing with raw materials and supplying finished goods to customers as well as handling returns.

Glossary

ASN

Advance Shipment Notice. An EDI formatted electronic packing list that is received by the consignee prior to receipt of the product. It can also include order information, product description, physical characteristics, type of packaging, marking, carrier information, and configuration data. In the EDI X12 system, it is known as the EDI 856 document.

Warehouse operations ensure that warehouses meet required levels of quality (on-time/in-full despatch as well as inventory holding accuracy) as cost effectively as possible.

ATP
Available To Promise. An advanced IT-enabled business process that provides the ability to promise stock to customers based on forecast production and demand as well as actual inventory on hand.

WMS
Warehouse Management System. A software package that controls the movement and storage of materials within a warehouse and processes the associated transactions, including receiving, put-away, picking, loading and despatch. More advanced systems allow real time control, visual management and facilities to optimise performance.

Value added activities
Value-added in the context of warehouse operations refers to non-standard activities that are possible to perform in the warehouse, beyond the normal receipt, pick pack, despatch process.

MHE
Material Handling Equipment. Equipment that is used for the movement, storage, control and protection of materials throughout the physical supply chain.

ERP

Enterprise Resource Planning. A system that is used to manage and coordinate all the resources, information, and functions of a business.

RF communication

Refers to the use of Radio Frequency communications with remote terminals that enable WMS records to be updated in real time and work instructions to be transmitted to operatives.

SOX

Refers to the provisions of the Sarbanes-Oxley act that applies to publicly listed companies in the USA. In this document we only refer to its requirements for internal control and disclosure where the intention is to provide rules and processes that prevent firms misstating their assets.

Cycle counting

Process by which stock levels are continually monitored removing the need for a periodic total stock take (subject to the business's financial controls). Each stock item has its own frequency of count and accuracy tolerance depending on criticality and value.

D3 Elements	Competency	Proficiency	Mastery
D3.1 Receive and put away stock	All deliveries are booked in by supplier giving pallet/outer quantity and purchase order numbers, with each vehicle having a delivery slot. On arrival product is blind checked and refused unless able to be matched back to a Purchase Order (PO). Any product without product data in the system is quarantined until it is measured/weighed. Random quality checks are completed on intake. Put-away location is allocated based on a comprehensive warehouse map on system with hierarchy of different storage location types.	There is a nominated carrier scheme for goods-in and use of outbound transport vehicles for supplier collections. All deliveries are booked in by supplier on an online system, giving full product list and quantities matched to PO. The number of unloading slots available is dynamic and is driven by inbound workload. There is a regular quality control and quarantine process including strict regulations on product packaging dimensions and presentation standards. There are mobile Radio Frequency (RF) terminals on Materials Handling Equipment (MHE) to confirm put away by scanning warehouse location barcode and there is real-time RF update on stock receipt. Product is put onto the system within 2 hours of receipt.	All deliveries are booked in by supplier on an online system using Advanced Shipping Notices (ASNs), giving full product list and quantities matched to PO. There is visibility of inbound shipment status by SKU and by purchase order which allows buyers to prioritise and automatically schedule in priority products. Upon arrival product is scanned and refused unless able to be matched back to a PO and product data is in the system. Put-away location is optimised according to algorithms linked to warehouse map which contribute to achieving higher utilisation of available storage space (target is 85% storage utilisation). The warehouse management system offers multiple location type options, dynamic pick face allocation with option for 'direct to pick face' and multi-locations per SKU (if necessary). Facility exists to put product straight onto stock without having to be put away (cross docking).

D3.2 Replenish stock	There is a review of empty picking faces before picking starts and replenishment takes place. Current stock availability levels are measured.	Product has to be in a storage location and on the system before it is available for picking. Pre-picking Available to Promise (ATP) checks are carried out and all locations replenished to ensure that sufficient product is in locations prior to picking to ensure pickers are not delayed. The warehouse has an independent monitoring mechanism of stock levels for tracking stock run rate and likely run out times. This covers stock in the warehouse and in transit and links this in with Planning function. Stock availability is measured and root cause analysis is undertaken to allow structured issue resolution. There is barcode control on replenishment locations.	Pre-picking ATP check covers both the warehouse and in transit stock. The system has the ability to cross dock incoming products and to manage receipts direct to pick face to bypass replenishment. Replenishment of pick faces during picking is driven by real-time RF updates. The replenishment system allows option for dynamic pick face allocation and can create multiple locations per SKU. The replenishment system has an option to select and clear near empty reserve stock locations. Layout allows picking to continue whilst replenishment is occurring (e.g. multiple zones, or at a time where no picking is taking place).
D3.3 Receive and schedule orders	There is a set cut off time for orders to be received to meet agreed loading time. A credit check happens prior to despatch. If product is unavailable, it is highlighted at the point of ordering and either put to backorder (with projected delivery date), or cancelled.	The ATP functionality reserves product for customer at the point of order, based on the availability of existing stock levels in the warehouse (start of day less product confirmed and orders taken). The RFP response includes pro formas (resources, productivity, cost) so that easy comparisons between competing bids can be made, and helps avoid contractor errors in data interpretation. Order cut off time leaves time for credit check to be carried out prior to picking starting. No orders are released to the warehouse without the credit check having been completed.	The ATP functionality can reserve stock in transit that can be turned around to meet lead-times. Where stock in transit is required for ATP, then customer services can highlight inbound vehicles to be prioritised for unloading. There are full records of cancelled orders and they are used to drive root cause analysis of reasons for product unavailability and to measure lost sales. Order cut off time leaves time for credit check to be carried out prior to picking starting, but credit checking is based on customer profiling. The order schedule is created on pick waves which optimises both staff capacity for picking and space constraints for marshalling, consolidation and loading for transport carriers despatch times.

(continued on next page)

D3 Elements

D3.4 Pick order for customer

Competency	Proficiency	Mastery
There is a clear order cut-off time and all picking is targeted to be finished by a set time to allow loading to start. Pick sequence is aligned to warehouse layout to minimise picking travel time. Individual orders can be picked by more than one picker and then product is consolidated. Overall productivity of warehouse shifts are measured (units per hour and picking accuracy). All locations are clearly marked (e.g. label, light, barcode, check digit).	Orders are picked in waves to meet planned despatch times. Picking faces have been replenished prior to picking starting. Orders are released for picking at the last possible day/time to ensure the delivery schedule is met, thereby maximising the product available to be picked. The productivity of individual pickers is measured. There is the ability to target (by product, picker or customer) sample checking of orders to measure pick accuracy. The level of sample checking is dictated by the accuracy available from the type of picking technology employed. An investigation is carried out into each discrepancy at pick.	Real-time visibility of pick wave or batch completion is available to supervisors. Pick sequence is aligned to warehouse layout and picking zones to minimise picking travel time and the system supports picking and put away dual cycling. The system supports multiple picking methods with optimisation algorithm (pick by order, bulk or batch picking, sweep picking). Appropriate technology is utilised (e.g. hand-held terminals for RF picking, voice controlled picking, pick by light etc.). Real-time RF update on picking system requires picker to confirm what has been picked before continuing. Shortages are automatically updated on invoices to allow near real-time monitoring of individual productivity/task completion. Orders are released for picking in waves and can be dynamically re-prioritised by supervisors to manage unforeseen changes in picking capacity, space constraints and despatch schedules.

D3.5 Manage value added operations	Value-added tasks are defined and managed as a discrete activity in a clearly defined work area.	Equipment and processes have been designed to optimise overall performance. Value-added activities are accounted for separately (cost and resources). There are specific and relevant performance measures in place for value-added activities.	The placement of value-adding processes within the supply chain is the result of a strategic end-to-end review. Within the warehouse, timing of value added activities is tied in with picking and despatch schedules. The system gives the ability to manage peaks by undertaking value added work to differing levels of completion and then put product to stock as a separate SKU. Performance management is in place including benchmarking vs. other (external and internal) operations.
D3.6 Manage delivery to customer	All loading starts at a set time. Product is picked to pre-designated despatch bays. Product is presented for loading in reverse delivery sequence for each vehicle. There is an end of shift review to ensure all of the product has been loaded and all loads despatched. Despatch and delivery documents are produced at the point of loading.	Picking and value added activity prioritisation is aligned to the despatch schedule. Vehicle loading is controlled in delivery sequence for earliest trailer departure times. Order confirmation updates stock records and the invoice is automatically produced in a batch run within 24 hours of despatch. There is an automatic system notification if the load is not confirmed by the expected despatch time.	Picking and value added activity is undertaken in waves to integrate with the despatch schedule. There is an automatic check weight calculation at the packing station for shipping documentation. There is real-time visibility of load consolidation in marshalling area to trigger trailer loading. Loading confirmation is by barcode scanning and despatch, and delivery documents are automatically generated as goods are packed and the invoice on confirmation of loading. Loading confirmation updates inventory and order status in real-time. Barcodes are used to track and trace despatch, linking stillages, pallets and crates to individual outers detailing order contents.

(continued on next page)

D3 Elements

D3.7 Manage inventory

Competency	Proficiency	Mastery
Annual stock takes (wall-to-wall) are performed, with a defined stock take process which is adhered to. Actual to book stock is reconciled prior to operations recommencing. Stock losses are allocated against specific budgets and clear targets set for acceptable levels of loss. A process exists to review excess and redundant stock.	Stock availability levels are measured and robust investigation is conducted on all stock discrepancies and remedial actions are put in place and monitored. Inventory rotation is by First-In-First-Out (FIFO), batch or lot. Cycle counting is used for continuous monitoring of inventory accuracy and checking is by location. The frequency of product checks varies according to rate of movement, value and level of shrinkage. There a clear split between overage stock and losses incurred through theft and damage. Discrepancies are investigated and remedial actions put in place.	Cycle counting is used and consistent high performance renders physical wall-to-wall stock checks redundant (99.8%+ item and location accuracy). Random perpetual inventory checking can be linked to picking routines. Rules exist to instigate wall-to-wall checks if cycle count results or frequency drop below key threshold levels. Count is by location and frequency is based on location accession frequency, SKU throughput, value and level of shrinkage. Functional access is SOX compliant, preventing individual members of staff from having the ability to access conflicting functions (typically receipting, counting and stock adjustment). Time stamps and user IDs are recorded for all stock transactions using RF equipment and bar code scanning. All users have unique IDs.

D3.8 Returns management

Returns authorisations are issued and scheduled back into the warehouse and held in quarantine prior to sortation. Clear rules exist as to what can be returned to stock and what needs to go for clearance or destruction. Logs are kept of returns activity.	Product requiring recalls can be traced back through the distribution network. Evidence of a logical business case is developed as to why returns are handled in the warehouse, which is reviewed periodically. All returns are tracked from point of despatch through to the point where they are returned to stock. Pre-advice is provided of returns and are scheduled back into warehouse with returns scanned on receipt and matched to approved returns authorisations. Returns are regarded as a stock item and stock data is used as input in planning replenishment.	Company sales policies minimises returns by recognising the non value added costs of making returns. Returns are treated as a supplier in their own right so that management attention is focused on returns. Clear productivity KPIs exist for processing returns and time targets exist to quickly place good stock back into inventory for resale. Tracking is used to prioritise handling of returns based on maximising sales potential. Returns reason code analysis is undertaken and used as input into policy/product development decisions to reduce returns, with close collaboration between Quality Control, Logistics and Buying.

Warehouse performance management ensures that warehouses meet required safety standards whilst using technology and staff capability to deliver improved performance.

Description

This profile applies to all operations which directly control warehousing and covers warehousing of all raw materials, WIP and finished goods.

Context

Warehousing is a critical element of the supply chain, with a significant impact on quality, costs and customer service since it plays a role in feeding manufacturing with raw materials and supplying finished goods to customers as well as handling returns.

Glossary

SLA

Abbreviation for a Service Level Agreement, an agreement between the supplying and receiving parties defining how the service is provided. At minimum this details service and quality levels, but it can cover every aspect of supply from cost, delivery, returns, innovation and improvement.

H&S

Health & Safety. A cross-disciplinary area concerned with protecting the safety, health and welfare of people engaged in work or employment as well as co-workers, family members, employers, customers, suppliers, nearby communities, and other members of the public who are impacted by the workplace environment.

PPE

Personal Protective Equipment, as used by warehouse staff to minimise risks of injury.

MHE

Material Handling Equipment. Equipment that is used for the movement, storage, control and protection of materials throughout the physical supply chain.

WMS

Warehouse Management System. A software package that controls the movement and storage of materials within a warehouse and processes the associated transactions, including receiving, put-away, picking, loading and despatch. More advanced systems allow real time control, visual management and facilities to optimise performance.

ERP

Enterprise Resource Planning. A system that is used to manage and coordinate all the resources, information, and functions of a business.

RF communication

Refers to the use of Radio Frequency communications with remote terminals that enable WMS records to be updated in real time and work instructions to be transmitted to operatives.

D4 Elements	Competency	Proficiency	Mastery
D4.1 **Manage health, safety and environment policy and regulatory requirements**	There is a warehouse Health, Safety and Environment (HSE) policy, which is adhered to. There are documented standards for storage and handling of different types of material as appropriate to their individual requirements. A risk based PPE (Personal Protective Equipment) policy is operated and enforced for all staff and visitors on the shop floor. An HSE and Material Handling Equipment (MHE) operational training programme exists and compliance is documented. A designated individual is responsible for ensuring all operating licenses are up-to-date and displayed as appropriate. There is controlled entry and access to facility with random checking of staff on exit.	Housekeeping standards are documented and communicated, including racking standards, MHE, cleanliness and tidiness, pallet quality, clear signage, well-marked walkways. Conformance to the Health and Safety (H&S) and housekeeping standards is monitored. A scheduled maintenance programme for MHE, doors, ramps and racking exists, with defined defecting procedures. MHE is taken out of service if safety defects are identified. The MHE operating standards are monitored and lapses acted upon. All incidents and near-misses are investigated and acted upon.	Individuals have responsibility for on-going housekeeping tasks as part of normal workload. The Health and Safety (H&S) statistics are monitored and subject to a continuous improvement process. The maintenance programme is scheduled to minimise MHE downtime and therefore overall resource required. Standards for MHE procurement, maintenance and operation include safety considerations.

D4.2 Systems and equipment	A stock control system is used in all warehouses, with inventory per SKU maintained per warehouse. Stock movement orders can be received electronically. Inventory per SKU is recorded per location. There is a single entry point and ownership for each data set. Manual procedures exist and have been tested as back up for all system activities. The MHE is suitable for the loads carried and is used appropriately to maximise operational safety.	Major activities are supported by the Warehouse Management System (WMS). The WMS is fully integrated with ERP system for order and stock control. The WMS supports labour planning and reporting as well as bar code scanning. The WMS supports batch and lot control with full traceability and staff member responsible for picking. There is a MHE service contract with Service Level Agreement (SLAs). The MHE is maintained with guaranteed response time and first fix rates in the event of breakdown.	All warehouses use WMS systems that are fully integrated with ERP and transport systems. The WMS functionality supports RF communication, bar code scanning, voice control and Radio-Frequency Identity as appropriate. The WMS allows for a choice of picking methodologies (e.g. order picking, batch picking, pick by line, zone picking). Picking is system-directed to balance efficiency with urgency. The labour planning, control and reporting are all performed using the WMS (or other integrated system) and the system automatically feeds a performance monitoring system to Full Time Equivalent (FTE) level. Systems have robust back-up processes in place including 'hot-swap' backup servers and 24/7 system support with guaranteed response time and uptime rates.
D4.3 Develop staff capabilities	A framework of skills and competencies for each role exists to identify basic training needs. Staff are given basic training in their designated role when recruited (e.g. operation of Material Handling Equipment, Health Safety Security and Environment, product recognition). Full records of training and qualification are kept.	Refresher training programmes are in place for all key trainings. The RFP response includes pro formas (resources, productivity, cost) so that easy comparisons between competing bids can be made, and helps avoid contractor errors in data interpretation.	Staff understand how their specific role and performance contributes to service fulfilment objectives and the impact on the wider operation of it not being completed properly. Metrics are used to monitor effectiveness of role specific training.

(continued on next page)

D4 Elements	Competency	Proficiency	Mastery
D4.4 Performance management	Warehouse cost and service levels are recorded on a monthly basis. Errors can be traced to staff. There is tiered responsibility for performance management though the command and control structure.	Warehouse productivity and service levels are monitored weekly against specific targets and action plans agreed. These plans span layout, working practices, technology and safety. Productivity and accuracy can be measured by activity, by operative, by day. Root cause analysis is used to improve productivity. All staff understand and can articulate recent performance and targets relevant to their role. Weekly meetings are held with different workgroups to review performance and league tables by shift/department are used to highlight performance issues as well as recognise success. There is detailed analysis of inventory accuracy and damage rates with weekly reviews and root cause analysis.	A daily 'dashboard' of core KPIs is made available to management, where (e.g. warehouse productivity, service levels, capacity utilisation, lead times and customer fulfilment, perfect order and damage levels) are monitored weekly against specific targets and action plans agreed. Key variable and service KPIs (including individual staff productivity) are available to management on a daily basis. The warehouse staff develop and implement improvement plans for the warehouse. Financial budgeting exercises use activity-based costing. Specific function targets are integrated with cross supply chain inventory, cost and service targets to optimise overall, end-to-end supply chain performance. A continuous improvement culture is encouraged amongst the staff groups and functions.

Transport operations covers the transport of all goods (raw materials, semi-finished and finished goods) between suppliers, manufacturing sites, warehouses and customers.

Description

Its objectives are to meet the service standards expected as cost effectively as possible. This profile applies to all operations that directly control transport, and covers transport of all raw materials, WIP and finished goods.

Context

Transport is a critical element of the supply chain, with a significant impact on costs and customer service. This profile measures how well transport is managed to achieve business requirements.

Glossary

ASN

Advance Shipment Notice. An EDI formatted electronic packing list that is received by the consignee prior to receipt of the product. It can also include order information, product description, physical characteristics, type of packaging, marking, carrier information, and configuration data. In the EDI X12 system, it is known as the EDI 856 document.

Warehouse performance management ensures that warehouses meet required safety standards whilst using technology and staff capability to deliver improved performance.

ATP

Available To Promise. An advanced IT-enabled business process that provides the ability to promise stock to customers based on forecast production and demand as well as actual inventory on hand.

D5 Elements	Competency	Proficiency	Mastery
D5.1 Mode optimisation	Orders are routed by mode and carrier according to well defined and communicated rules.	A number of different transport/vehicle options are available (e.g. road, express road, air) to meet different requirements of urgency, cost and order size as appropriate to customer needs. A clear policy exists on the preferred transport mode based on minimising end-to-end cost whilst meeting service levels. The choice of transport mode, carrier and route is system controlled taking into account despatch time, delivery time, consignment weight and dimensions, product specific requirements, handling requirements, insurance, security and service level.	Optimisation capability exists to select the preferred option to meet the trade-off of service versus cost. There is regular liaison with the planning team to address issues where upstream supply chain delays cause unnecessary use of express transport. Where selection differs from the policy, the reasons are investigated and the excess cost charged back to the responsible department.

(continued on next page)

D5 Elements	Competency	Proficiency	Mastery
D5.2 Routing and scheduling	A delivery schedule is available, defining routings for each vehicle. Master data is updated as new information is received.	Vehicle scheduling is computerised and is seen as a core competency. Routes are re-calculated at least monthly. Orders are scheduled to meet customer delivery requirements. Vehicle scheduling parameters include customer specific restrictions, vehicle restrictions, driver hours, road speeds, product types, reloading, nights out and multi-depot. Scheduling takes place across product flows (e.g. inbound and outbound, primary and secondary, or customer deliveries and returns). A nominated individual has responsibility for ensuring master data (e.g. customer specific requirements and constraints, lead times, capacities, calendars and priorities) is accurate. System parameters are regularly reviewed, fine-tuned and updated.	Vehicle scheduling is computerised and dynamic based on real-time GPS data where a route plan can be updated in real-time and communicated to vehicles. Backorders and late changes to the distribution plan can be added to existing orders where feasible. There is capability to pre-advise of delivery online to the customer once the route schedule is confirmed. Inbound schedules are linked to outbound schedules to facilitate backloads, reload opportunities and factory gate options. On time delivery alert is available to customers using GPS and geofencing technology.
D5.3 Inter-site transport	Each location is responsible for arranging their own inter-site despatches. Inter-site loads are expedited based on product availability in an ad hoc manner.	There is a structured approach to managing inter-site loads based on current and forecast availability.	A single control point is used to optimise backloads and vehicle fill.

	Internal movement orders are produced and a lead-time exists for transfers to be completed within. Inbound delivery performance is recorded (inbound OTIF), and a booking-in schedule is operated for goods-in.	The RFP response includes pro formas (resources, productivity, cost) so that easy comparisons between competing bids can be made, and helps avoid contractor errors in data interpretation. Pre-advice is sent between sites which can be received and processed to streamline goods-in. System stock transfer is driven by physical delivery confirmation at receiving site, not automatic. Loads not booked in within 24 hours of receipt are flagged on the system.	Inter-site schedules (and schedule changes) are integrated with manufacturing planning and Available-to-Promise (ATP). Core inter-site activity is run on a standard timetable flattened as far as possible throughout the week which is reviewed seasonally. Inter-site loads have fixed delivery windows. Additional loads are scheduled as required and Customer Services can prioritise loads based on stock availability and customer demand for products. Pre-advice Advanced Shipping Notices (ASN) are received and processed to streamline goods-in for all inter-site deliveries. Inter-site transport is treated as any supplier (e.g. if a delivery slot is missed, a vehicle will not automatically be unloaded).
D5.4 Customer service management (continued on next page)	Service level and delivery days are agreed with the customer. Both Customers and Sales talk directly to schedulers if a change is wanted to the delivery schedule. Returns are collected when presented without pre-advice. Monthly performance reporting is provided to the customer. The Customer directs all non-schedule delivery queries through Customer Services with ad hoc issue resolution of service problems.	A process exists to allow unattended deliveries at pre-agreed delivery points. All requests by customer/sales force for schedule changes are directed through customer services, not direct to schedulers. Performance against target lead-time are measured. Root cause analysis of delivery issues takes place with joint responsibility to address them. Pre-delivery notification is via Short Message Service (SMS) or through a customer on-line portal, where customers can track delivery status via track and trace. A clear communications process in place to pre-advise customers of deliveries that will fail and product shortages.	There is on-going work with customers to manage the delivery windows and days to flatten the week. There is a documented seasonal planning process that works with customers/outlets to pull deliveries forward at peak times and with demand/supply planning to match stock availability to the schedule. Flexible vehicle fleet capacity is used to manage peaks and troughs by subcontractors, back haulage and out of hours/night trunking. The process is based on optimising total cost to deliver whilst satisfying service levels.

D5 Elements	Competency	Proficiency	Mastery
D5.5 Fleet maintenance	Accurate fleet records are maintained including identification marks, equipment type, age, date acquired, finance status and location.	The maintenance operation is set up to obtain maximum utilisation of the fleet assets and minimise downtime.	Vehicles are checked on their return for minor defects and fixed prior to next shift starting, so minimising downtime.

Deliver

D6 Transport performance management

Transport performance management ensures that transport operations meet required safety standards whilst using the fleet, staff capabilities and technology to deliver improved performance.

Description

This profile applies to all operations which directly control transport, and covers transport of all raw materials, WIP and finished goods.

Context

Transport is a critical element of the supply chain, with a significant impact on costs and customer service. This profile measures how well transport is managed to achieve business requirements.

Glossary

H&S

Health & Safety. A cross-disciplinary area concerned with protecting the safety, health and welfare of people engaged in work or employment as well as co-workers, family members, employers, customers, suppliers, nearby communities, and other members of the public who are impacted by the workplace environment.

Transport performance management ensures that transport operations meet required safety standards whilst using the fleet, staff capabilities and technology to deliver improved performance.

PPE
Personal Protective Equipment, as used by warehouse staff to minimise risks of injury.

POD
Proof of Delivery, can take two principal forms (1) a 'soft copy' which is the data of name, date and time and possibly also a scanned signature file (2) a 'hard copy' which is an actual signed delivery note (or sometimes a fax copy of it).

D6 Transport performance management

D6 Elements	Competency	Proficiency	Mastery
D6.1 Fleet asset management	There are clear vehicle specifications and procurement standards.	There are clear procurement standards based on lifetime costs.	The organisation obtains the lowest total operating cost for its fleet. This is achieved through balancing subcontractors and own account fleets, plus innovative use of service acquisition, fleet sharing and full understanding of lifetime costs.
D6.2 Manage health, safety and environment policy and regulatory requirements	There is a transport standards policy aligned with local legislation (e.g. vehicles, insurance, tax, drivers hours). All collisions, incidents and injuries are investigated. Management of MOT's, servicing schedule and all other licences are the responsibility of a nominated individual. Vehicle defecting procedures are defined, followed and audited. Vehicles are taken out of service if unsafe to operate. Driver standards are monitored and lapses reviewed with the driver.	Transport policies and procedures are regularly audited and enforced as required. The Health and Safety (H&S) statistics are monitored and all incidents are investigated and acted upon. The H&S statistics are subject to a continuous improvement process. Standard driver Personal Protective Equipment (PPE) is provided and its use is rigorously enforced. Pre and post journey debriefing is in place. Driver lapses are treated as a serious disciplinary matter and drivers' hours legislation is scrupulously followed.	Management of MOT's, servicing schedule and all other licences are system supported. Standards of equipment procurement, maintenance and operation are designed to meet the transport safety targets of the organisation. Vehicle defecting uses in-cab or mobile computing. Hazard spot mapping and permitted night stop places are in place (supported by vehicle tracking). There are certain 'non-negotiable' rules that result in immediate disciplinary action (e.g. use of telephones whilst driving; driving without seatbelts; exceeding driving hours without permission).

(continued on next page)

D6 Elements	Competency	Proficiency	Mastery
D6.3 Systems	There is systemised reconciliation of journeys, loads and carrier payments with batch file transfer. Systems are fully integrated if more than one system is used. Manual procedures exist and have been tested as back up for all system activities. A fleet management system is in place that controls the maintenance of fleet as well as recording its location, ownership and finance status.	The organisation employs systems to route consignments, monitor consignment status en-route (track and trace), collect Proof of Delivery (POD) information and schedule resources. The RFP response includes pro formas (resources, productivity, cost) so that easy comparisons between competing bids can be made, and helps avoid contractor errors in data interpretation. A fleet management system is in place that controls the acquisition, maintenance and disposal of fleet as well as recording its location, ownership and finance status.	Vehicles are scheduled dynamically (via GPS). A POD imaging capability is available together with web portal interface for customers to monitor shipment progress. Transport planning system manages trailer and yard capacity. Engine monitoring systems and telematics measure driving efficiency. There is system enabled capacity management with 3rd parties for load sharing, backhaul, subcontracting.
D6.4 Documentation	There is a clear and documented process for creating delivery documentation. There is a formal process in place to ensure that documentation required for deliveries is complete and accurate, including checks if necessary.	The documentation process is regularly audited and audit results are acted upon. There are reports available showing error rates for documentation.	All documentation errors are collated and analysed for root causes and actions are taken to eliminate issues.

D6.5 Develop staff capabilities	A framework of skills and competencies for each role exists to identify basic training needs. Staff are given basic training in their designated role when recruited (e.g. for drivers Health, Safety, Security and Environment training, product recognition, customer service and a practical driving test). Full records of training and qualification are kept.	Refresher training programmes are in place for all key trainings. Scheduling and customer service staff are cross trained so they can work in each other's departments. A continuous improvement culture is encouraged.	Defensive driving and fatigue management form part of the core courses for training. Driver mentors are used to provide on-going assessment of driver capability. Scheduling operations are centralised to give economies of scale that facilitate career development, process standardisation, continuous training. Specific metrics are used to monitor effectiveness of role specific training.
D6.6 Performance management	Transport costs and service levels are recorded. There are clear targets and KPIs for transport costs and service.	There is a structured performance management approach that includes cost and service levels as well as cost drivers. Targets are set and reviewed on a regular basis by different modes of transport and channels to market. There is a clear link between KPIs and reward mechanism. Adjustments to performance are linked back to transport capacity plans and routing and scheduling systems. Root cause analysis is undertaken on all service failures, by driver, product, customer and route. There is a demonstrable continuous improvement process with targets and improvement focus areas being set.	The performance management process is audited and system enabled, supporting a drill-down into the cost drivers. Cost and profit can be managed at the level of a vehicle (truck, ship, plane etc.) with planned and actual contract costs monitored. Budgets are set using activity based costing and cost to serve is an input into operational decisions. Steps have been taken to mitigate the impact of fuel price variation including bulk buying, bunkering and hedging. Scheduling effectiveness and driver variance to planned route is measured by comparing cost of actual schedule with the optimal, planned system schedule.

D7 Contractor management

Contractor management ensures that outsourced service providers (transport and/or warehousing) provide the required performance levels and value for money.

Description

This profile applies to all operations that manage contracts and relationships with outsourced logistics service providers (3PLs, 4PLs or LLPs). The profile covers contractors working in all areas of transport and warehousing, for all types of material - inbound raw materials, WIP and finished products.

Context

Transport and warehousing is a critical element of the supply chain, with a significant impact on costs and customer service. How the relationship with the provider of these services is managed is consequently important. This profile is linked with the 'Warehouse management' and 'Transport management' profiles (which typically describe the functions that the service provider operates), as well as the 'Network design and management' profile since the service provider could be significantly inputting to these activities.

Deliver

D7 Contractor management

Contractor management ensures that outsourced service providers (transport and/or warehousing) provide the required performance levels and value for money.

Glossary

WMS

Warehouse Management System. A software package that controls the movement and storage of materials within a warehouse and processes the associated transactions, including receiving, put-away, picking, loading and despatch. More advanced systems allow real time control, visual management and facilities to optimise performance.

3PL

Abbreviation for a 3rd Party Logistics provider which is a specialist provider of transport and/or warehousing services. They may also carry out other tasks such as order taking.

LLP / 4PL

Abbreviation for a Lead Logistics Provider. This is a specialist form of 3PL, which will manage a large scale distribution operation and sub-contract elements to other 3PLs as required and effective. They will generally also take more responsibility for overall optimisation of the distribution network. The key advantage is that only a single contractual relationship needs managing.

Contractor management ensures that outsourced service providers (transport and/or warehousing) provide the required performance levels and value for money.

RFP
Abbreviation for Request For Proposal, used at the tendering part of the sourcing process to formalise each supplier's proposal for meeting the company's requirements.

SLA
Abbreviation for a Service Level Agreement, an agreement between the supplying and receiving parties defining how the service is provided. At minimum this details service and quality levels, but it can cover every aspect of supply from cost, delivery, returns, innovation and improvement.

D7 Elements	Competency	Proficiency	Mastery
D7.1 Contracting strategy	The organisation has decided which services to outsource (e.g. regions, services, modes, asset provision) based on a clear rationale. A communication strategy with the relevant operational managers and staff affected has been agreed.	Outsourcing decisions are based upon a strategic evaluation of the core competencies of the organisation, customer requirements and the value-added potential of third parties (e.g. cost reduction, new service capabilities, more flexible capacity), such that outsourcing will not conflict with any future, longer term business strategy. Known performance issues in the operation are addressed prior to outsourcing, so that the efficiencies are gained by the internal organisation rather than the contractor. The decision to outsource or not includes cost and capability hurdles.	Outsourcing decision recognises that the contractor's management fee is justifiable such that the overall solution is provided at lower cost (or better service) then current operation (e.g. superior purchasing power for asset prices, better use of technology and economies of scale of operation/ network). There is a clear decision of whether any strategic assets need to be kept in-house if the transfer of these to a contractor might represent a risk to the business (e.g. ownership of warehouse, WMS, or vehicle fleet). The strategy considers all the different routes to market, and the most cost-effective way to serve these and achieve lowest end-to-end, supply chain cost. The contracting strategy decision process has been completed within the last 3 years.

D7 Elements	Competency	Proficiency	Mastery
D7.2 RFP preparation and issue	The Request For Proposal (RFP) specification of requirements includes information on the operation, service levels, safety requirements, and volumes/data which the contractors will require. The RFP includes a draft legal 'Heads of Agreement' so that contractors can respond to significant, legal issues as identified, including contractors obligations and guarantees, liabilities, transfer of employees or assets/property leases.	The RFP gives detailed explanation of Service Level Agreements (SLAs) and KPIs that require to be satisfied, and contractors are asked to respond where they have proven capabilities in these areas. The RFP gives guidance on the type of commercial terms required, whether open book or closed book, and fixed or variable management fee, with clear definitions for the components of the management fee. Contractors are selected following a tender process that was completed within the last 3-5 years that includes a wide range of contractors that have been pre-selected from desktop research or via a structured Request for Information exercise. A full range of Lead Logistics Providers (LLP), Fourth-Party Logistics Provider (4PL) and Third-Party Logistics Provider (3PL) options are considered.	The RFP is not prescriptive of the solution required, so that the contractor brings both technical and commercial added value to its design by responding to the defined service levels required. The organisation understands why the charging mechanism (open book or closed book, and management fee) was selected and takes measures to mitigate the risks associated with it. The organisation understands whether their contract is 'transactional' or 'value adding', and therefore understands the links between contract length, contractor risk, and the level of management fee that contractors will likely require. The RFP commercial terms has part of the contractor's management fee linked to performance with both incentives and penalties, and that the contractor is not incentivised to hit a service level that is not needed. Contractors are required to demonstrate continuous improvement with a commitment to on-going cost reduction, with the contract having incentives so that the contractor is proactive and shares in the reward.

D7.3 Contractor evaluation and selection

At least three quotes are obtained for all contracted services. Contractors are selected following a tender process that gives potential suppliers a clear understanding of the service required. The organisation holds signed contracts for all contracted services. Evaluation criteria are agreed internally by the stakeholders, and contractors are asked to answer how their response has met these criteria.	The RFP contains concise detail on the operational processes, activities, service levels required so that the contractor cannot subsequently seek cost increases for activities that were not specified in the original RFP. The RFP response includes pro formas (resources, productivity, cost) so that easy comparisons between competing bids can be made, and helps avoid contractor errors in data interpretation. The evaluation process includes face-to-face meetings/presentations, and visits to reference sites which helps prove capability and cultural fit. Contractors are assessed against each other and where appropriate potential in-house operation (consistent with the outsourcing strategy).	An activity model is developed prior to tendering to understand the size of the opportunities which may result from the contracting process. A contract costing structure is developed to ensure that key cost drivers are understood and are visible, which also helps focus on the development of productivity improvements, innovation and cost sharing. Contractors and any potential in-house operation (consistent with the outsourcing strategy) are assessed against each other with a clearly defined set of criteria including cost of change and capability hurdles.

D7 Elements

D7.4 Contractor performance management

Competency	Proficiency	Mastery
Contractor performance is monitored for both cost and service. Contractors submit performance reports on time and in line with their SLAs. Review meetings have minutes with resulting action plans monitored.	A joint implementation plan is developed and monitored, with clear responsibilities for implementation, resources, IT systems scope and costs. There is a formal, tiered review process that allows for operational, tactical and strategic matters to be discussed at appropriate levels within both organisations. Client management does not abdicate its responsibilities because the operation is outsourced, with continued focus required on cost reviews, budgets, volume forecasts, promotional activity, and analysis of variations. Seasonal volume and resource planning is jointly undertaken, and not left to the contractor alone. A clear remediation process exists. Mechanisms are in place to incentivise good performance and penalise poor performance.	There is a plan to over-manage the start-up if the implementation is of a new contract, with daily/weekly reviews of service until operation is stable, and with root cause analysis of issues. A clear contract plan is developed annually with jointly agreed targets for cost and service improvements built in, and a route map of the initiatives to achieve these improvements. Joint contract management meetings have formal agendas, including solving operational issues, reviewing KPIs and service issues for non-conformance, costs and comparisons to annualised budget, innovation agenda for improvement opportunities, and current issues and actions outstanding. Contractors and the organisation take joint responsibility for continuous improvement. The organisation has designated, trained contract managers in place, whose reward is linked to contractor performance.

Deliver

D8 Sustainability in delivery

Sustainability in delivery covers the operation of all owned warehouse and transport activities, as well as the management of service providers' operations.

Description
This profile applies to all internal logistics operations and to management of the services provided by third parties, and covers management of the sustainable operation of all company owned warehouse and transportation assets. It also covers the contract management activity relating to external provision of similar services which do not directly employ company assets.

Context
The physical assets used to store and move materials and finished products are some of the most visible elements of the company's operations. They have potentially significant impacts (both environmental and social) on the neighbourhoods in which they are located and the transport networks through which they pass.

Glossary
3PL

Abbreviation for a 3rd Party Logistics provider, which is a specialist provider of transport and/or warehousing services. They may also carry out other tasks such as order taking.

D8 Elements	Competency	Proficiency	Mastery
D8.1 Sustainability in warehousing	All sites conduct basic risk and impact assessments covering environmental, ethical and social aspects of operations.	All assessments are reported beyond Site Manager level and action plans to reduce impacts and risks are in place and monitored. Carbon footprint is measured and reported. The Warehouse team gets targets for improving environmental performance from company sustainability strategy, with the Logistics Director owning these targets.	Driving operational efficiency is used as a key tool in reducing the carbon footprint. A formal process in in place to share best practice across sites. A full through-life plan is produced for any new warehouse site, or extension, before operations begin. Action plans are in place to actively manage carbon footprint.
D8.2 Sustainability in transport	Sustainability policy and guidance in place covering procurement and use of all transport assets, for both product and personnel movements.	Impact assessments are carried out for all significant transport modes and routes. Action plans exist to reduce future impacts, including fleet management activities, modal shift options and route/service level redesign. Carbon footprint is measured and reported. The Transport team gets targets for improving environmental performance from company sustainability strategy, with the Logistics Director owning these targets. Data collection and reporting is automated to ensure consistency.	Driving operational efficiency is used as a key tool in reducing the carbon footprint. End-to-end supply chain models are used to optimise and reduce transportation impacts across all inbound, internal and outbound flows. Action plans are in place to actively manage carbon footprint. All assessments are reported beyond local manager level and action plans to reduce impacts and risks are in place and monitored.

D8.3 Sustainability in 3PL/4PL contracts	All new logistics service contracts are evaluated based on criteria which include sustainability impacts as well as service and financial criteria.	All new contracts and extensions include requirements to report against environmental metrics. The RFP response includes pro formas (resources, productivity, cost) so that easy comparisons between competing bids can be made, and helps avoid contractor errors in data interpretation. The Transport team gets targets for improving environmental performance from company sustainability strategy, with the Logistics Director owning these targets. Data collection and reporting is automated to ensure consistency.	3PLs and 4PLs sign up to deliver their part of the company's sustainability strategy. Sustainability is an important KPI and this is a key part of penalty/reward, investment criteria and renewal decisions.
D8.4 Regulatory compliance	There is an understanding of the most relevant legal frameworks.	There is a comprehensive understanding of the relevant legal frameworks in all operating territories together with excellent compliance. There is an active approach to regulatory compliance.	There is a high level of awareness about planned regulatory changes and there are plans in place to prepare for these. The organisation plays a part in shaping future policy through active engagement.

Demand

- Demand forecasting
- Demand management
- Customer relationship management
- Sales order processing
- Customer & channel segmentation
- New product development
- Promotion planning
- Sustainability in demand

6 Demand

Demand is the function that manages the customer interface and the demand signal. It brings together an understanding of what the customer wants and defines the required service and channel offerings to meet customer needs. This function also forecasts, receives and shapes customer demand, passing this on to the rest of the supply chain.

The more strategic elements of Demand manage customer relationships, service definition, and how different customer groups are served. These processes enable a business to achieve target revenue and profitability through prioritising customers, channels and products.

Working with customers is a key part of this process, covered in customer relationship management. Discovering and defining real customer needs is a critical feed into developing compelling and profitable service propositions. Tracking how well a company is meeting the needs of each of its customers is important feedback for the rest of the supply chain.

In customer and channel segmentation, services and supply models are differentiated according to needs and characteristics of different customer groupings, to maximise leverage from supply resources and maximise customer satisfaction. New product development covers the management of product ranges, balancing costs and complexity against customer needs. It also covers simplification through design and standardisation of material inputs.

Demand forecasting is responsible for feeding an accurate and timely demand signal to the rest of the supply chain. Demand management aligns demand with financial targets, and shapes it to best fit the supply organisation. Promotion planning ensures that promotions are effective, with high availability and minimal write-offs, and do not cause unnecessary disruption through the supply chain.

Sales order processing is a critical interface with customers. Excellence requires full information on credit positions, stock availability, alternative products and up-selling options. There are critical interfaces with finance functions for payment collection, and with Deliver on product delivery requirements.

Sustainability in demand covers the environmental impact of product labelling and packaging. These areas are subject to regulation and legislation, and careful management can significantly improve their sustainability profile.

Demand

S1 Demand forecasting

Demand forecasting develops an unconstrained forecast of end customer demand, providing input into the demand and supply planning processes.

Description

This profile applies to forecasting end customer demand for all sales channels and products. The key output is an unconstrained forecast of end customer demand, based on the sales and marketing activities as defined in the demand plan.

Context

The demand forecast is the starting point for all supply chain planning, and the accuracy of the forecast is a key driver of supply chain performance. Inaccurate forecasts require buffering with additional inventory or manufacturing capacity, and may lead to out of stocks and service level failures.

S1 Elements	Competency	Proficiency	Mastery
S1.1 Single set of forecast data	There is a single set of demand forecast data in the business.	The demand forecast is based on the best estimate of future sales, rather than financial or sales budgets. The forecast includes all products and sales channels. The forecast includes products which are still in development and due to launch within the next 12 months.	The single set of forecast data drives all planning and financial processes with weekly/monthly updates. The single set of forecast data is visible and available to all functions which require it.
S1.2 Process and governance	There is a documented forecasting process used throughout the business unit. Any changes to the forecast are always approved formally as part of the Sales and Operations Planning (S&OP) process.	The most senior Sales or Marketing person in the business unit has full accountability for the ownership and governance of the demand plan. A formal programme is in place to train those involved in forecasting.	There is a regular audit of the forecasting process for compliance and process improvement.
S1.3 Forecasting granularity	Demand forecasts are updated at least every month. Demand forecasts are by SKU for the whole market.	Forecasts are by week for at least the first 12 weeks. The RFP response includes pro formas (resources, productivity, cost) so that easy comparisons between competing bids can be made, and helps avoid contractor errors in data interpretation.	Demand forecasts are by SKU, and by sales region, and regional warehouse to enable distribution planning. Demand forecasts are updated weekly, with a full re-forecast monthly.

S1.4 Clean history	At least 12 months' sales and forecast history is captured and analysed to understand sales events and trends. The seasonality profile is well understood as a key driver of sales patterns.	At least 2 years' sales and forecast history is captured and analysed to understand sales events and trends. All 'extraordinary' demand history is removed based on known events and drivers such as price changes, out of stocks, or competitor activity. There is a single 'baseline' forecast, and assumptions are documented within the forecasting system against every event removed.	At least 3 years' sales and forecast history is captured and analysed to understand sales events and trends. The impacts of historical sales events are captured for use in modelling similar future events.
S1.5 Forecasting approach	Sales event history is captured so that the drivers can be analysed. Collaboration with key customers is a standard part of the forecasting process. Key forecasting assumptions are documented. Different forecasting techniques adopted based on variability, volume and value. Baseline trend data is analysed, including cyclical and seasonality effects.	The demand plan includes input on market and competitor activity. Promotional demand is considered as uplift to base demand. Potential demand cannibalisation effects between related SKUs are identified and factored into forecasts. Different channels have been identified and are forecast separately. Bottom-up forecasts are validated against top-down forecasts using market insight data on size and share of overall market. External factors (e.g. competitor activity, weather) are included in forecast process and the assumptions are documented.	There is full understanding of which elements of the sales forecast drive specific supply chain planning decisions. Forecast accuracy measurements are aligned with key decision lead times. Promotional demand models are used to determine the shape of sales uplift based on previous promotions. Forecasts are expressed as an upper and lower limit and the underlying assumptions for each are documented and implications and actions for each identified.
S1.6 Monitoring and exception management	Forecasts are monitored as actual sales are reported. Any SKUs which have variances outside of the expected range are investigated further to identify the root cause of the variance.	Forecasts are monitored at least weekly as actual sales are reported. There are documented guidelines and targets (accuracy and bias) in place to investigate root causes of significant variances from the forecast. Bias and stability of forecast are measured at various lags. Forecast accuracy is formally reported as part of the demand planning and S&OP process.	There is a documented escalation path for forecast issues, culminating in the S&OP review. Bias and stability of forecast are measured at various lags.

(continued on next page)

S1 Elements	Competency	Proficiency	Mastery
S1.7 Systems	Forecast data is held on suitable systems, which interface with other systems.	The forecasting systems are fully integrated with other inventory planning systems. Systems can store all assumptions made against each forecast.	The systems enable online collaboration with customers to receive input on forecasts.
S1.8 Promotions	There is systematic forecast of promotions based on similar products and events. Collaboration with key customers is a standard part of the forecasting process and key assumptions are documented.	Input on market and competitor activity is used to adjust forecasts. Promotions are deployed in tester markets where possible to help predict sales before full roll-out. Potential demand cannibalisation effects are identified and factored into the forecast.	All promotional demands are well noted in sales history, so the sales uplifts can be removed from the baseline forecast. Forecasts are adjusted daily based on 'sales so far'. Post promotion reviews drive continual improvement of promotional activity.
S1.9 NPI (new product introduction)	New product forecasts are based on similar products and events. Systems are designed to handle NPI through retaining historical event data.	The regular evaluation of all NPI forecasts drives improvements in the forecasting process. The NPI milestone achievement is monitored by the S&OP process.	A specific collaboration process is in place with trading partners on NPI forecasts. The NPI forecasts are expressed as a range of outcomes with implications and actions for each range extreme identified.

Demand

S2 Demand management

Demand management aligns and confirms sales and marketing plans with demand forecasts and aligns demand plans with S&OP output.

Description

Demand management is the process which ensures that the overall sales plan is aligned with the demand forecasts, is coherent and makes best use of available resources, and shapes demand as required to fit with any supply constraints as governed by the S&OP process.

Context

Demand management is closely aligned with the demand forecasting process, the two processes work iteratively to develop an overall demand plan with agreed forecasts.

S2 Demand management

S2 Elements	Competency	Proficiency	Mastery
S2.1 Planning cycle and process	There is a documented demand/sales management process with formal monthly meetings. Standardised document formats are used to structure the monthly demand management process.	The demand management process has involvement from Supply Chain, Finance and Sales/Marketing. The process produces a documented sales plan which aligns with the demand forecast. The sales plan includes promotional and new product activity, or new customer acquisition.	The process defines guidelines for managing and shaping demand, and making optimal use of Sales and Marketing resources. The process is reviewed on a regular basis leading to process improvements.
S2.2 Integration with forecasting	The demand/sales management process is fully integrated with the forecasting process. The forecast accurately reflects all sales and marketing activities.	There is a single set of demand and financial forecasts which are aligned with the demand/sales plan. Any variations/shortfalls against financial or volume targets are noted and discussed as part of the review process.	The demand plan is used to develop financial projections of sales revenues, cash flow, and profit margins. The assumptions upon which the demand plan is based are monitored, reviewed and updated at least monthly. The Senior Demand Executives focus on the strategy required to narrow gaps between the demand plan revenue and the sales revenue objective in the business plan.

S2.3 Alignment with S&OP processes and outputs	The Sales and Operations Planning (S&OP) outputs are considered within the demand management process.	The RFP response includes pro formas (resources, productivity, cost) so that easy comparisons between competing bids can be made, and helps avoid contractor errors in data interpretation. The projection of revenue generated by the demand plan is compared each month to the sales revenue objective stated in the business plan. Outputs of the demand management process work to align demand with supply constraints.	The assumptions upon which the demand plan is based are monitored, reviewed and updated at least monthly. The demand planning process develops the financial projections of cash flow and profit margins as an input to the S&OP process.

S3 Customer relationship management

Customer relationship management is the process by which customer needs are established, performance tracked against targets, and improvements agreed which will benefits both parties.

Description

This profile covers the elements of customer contact relevant to assessing, satisfying and improving service levels. It does not cover any other sales and marketing processes.

Context

Customer satisfaction is a key supply chain objective, with significant impact on business growth and profitability. Customer relationship management is focused on establishing the key elements of customer satisfaction, and monitoring performance against those factors.

Glossary

SLA

Abbreviation for a Service Level Agreement, an agreement between the supplying and receiving parties defining how the service is provided. At its most basic, an SLA details service and quality levels, but can cover every aspect of supply from cost, delivery, returns, innovation and improvement.

CRM

Abbreviation for Customer Relationship Management.

S3 Customer relationship management

S3 Elements	Competency	Proficiency	Mastery
S3.1 Process, roles and responsibilities	There is a defined process for managing the relationship with customers, with specific roles also defined.	There is a focus on exception management and medium to long term (3-24 months) planning and process improvement. One of the main focuses of the Customer Relationship Management (CRM) process is to improve overall inter-company transactional and planning processes. There is a focus on the customers who generate the majority of volume/value/profit and/or are strategic to the business.	For strategically important customers the aim is to achieve a partnership through understanding each other's needs and constraints. There is a named role who is the overall owner of the account plan and Service Level Agreement (SLA) with strategic customers.
S3.2 Measurement and review	The agreed customer service levels which cover service and quality are well communicated. Customer satisfaction is gathered.	The success of customer relationship management is measured through SLA criteria. The SLA criteria are measured monthly to drive action plans where achievement falls short of target. There is a customer feedback process which is considered whilst creating customer relationship action plans.	Formal standardised surveys are used to assess customer satisfaction across a range of areas such as; service level, responsiveness, communication. Customer surveys are measured regularly and action plans put in place where satisfaction reduces or does not meet the required target. Customer feedback is used to develop the overall customer offering, service offering and product developments.

S3.3 Information management	Key data for customer accounts is held in one place and is regularly updated.	Key customer issues are documented and well communicated amongst the customer-facing team and if relevant across the organisation. The RFP response includes pro formas (resources, productivity, cost) so that easy comparisons between competing bids can be made, and helps avoid contractor errors in data interpretation.	All customer contact information is immediately available to all staff with customer contact. Requirements of key/strategic customers are well communicated and understood across the organisation.
S3.4 Communication	Customer service contact methods are defined.	There is more than one channel available for customer contact, for example call centre and e-mail.	Multiple channels are available for customer contact (e.g. call centre, web forms, e-mail). Customer enquiries are responded to within a day.

Sales order management defines how customer orders are managed, tracked, analysed and processed to maximise information on quality and minimise costs.

Description

This profile applies to end customer orders only, internal orders are covered by the 'Finished goods replenishment planning' profile. The scope includes managing and tracking customer orders, managing product returns and defective goods.

Context

End customer orders and returns represent an important link in the supply chain, with significant impact on customer service. Managing customer orders well minimises errors in order capture, and provides information to enable service deficiencies to be quickly identified and rectified, listing the key elements of customer satisfaction, and monitoring performance against those factors.

Glossary

ATP

Available To Promise. An advanced IT-enabled business process that provides the ability to promise stock to customers based on forecast production and demand as well as actual inventory on hand.

EDI

Electronic Data Interchange (EDI) refers to the structured transmission of data between organisations by electronic means. Or, more precisely, "the computer-to-computer interchange of strictly formatted messages that represent documents other than monetary instruments. Human intervention in the processing of a received message is typically intended only for error conditions."

ASN

Advance Shipment Notice. An EDI formatted electronic packing list that is received by the consignee prior to receipt of the product. It can also include order information, product description, physical characteristics, type of packaging, marking, carrier information, and configuration data. In the EDI X12 system, it is known as the EDI 856 document.

CRM

Abbreviation for Customer Relationship Management.

S4 Elements	Competency	Proficiency	Mastery
S4.1 Order receipt	Orders are captured in an integrated system. Orders inconsistent with logistics lead times are not accepted. All orders are credit checked.	The customer is informed of their order number and delivery date. Orders can be received by Electronic Data Interchange (EDI) or other electronic channels. Person to person order taking process includes facilities for up selling, incentivising and adjusting to logistically efficient configurations.	Orders are subjected to exception and error checking including against historical order patterns. An Available To Promise (ATP) process is in place for all ordering methods to ensure that firm delivery dates can be promised.
S4.2 Order fulfilment	Invoices are raised for all orders. Proof of delivery is available if required. All orders can be traced to a particular carrier and mode of transport.	Proof of delivery is available within 24 hours if required. Despatch confirmation and delivery confirmation are all automatically available depending on customer requirements.	Pre-advice and Advanced Shipping Notification (ASN) are automatically available depending on customer requirements. There are customer specific rules in place to respond to inventory availability issues.
S4.3 Late payment and credit control	Late payments are reviewed at least on a monthly basis, with any customer issues being actioned out of this monthly activity.	There are clear 'overdue payment' policy that is handled by a department/sub-group of staff. The RFP response includes pro formas (resources, productivity, cost) so that easy comparisons between competing bids can be made, and helps avoid contractor errors in data interpretation.	There is a differentiated late payment policy for different customer types, amounts and period overdue. Charges and interest levels can be set at various levels depending on the level of overdue payments.

S4.4 Cash and banking	Cash received can be reconciled to customer orders.	Cash received can be reconciled to customer orders electronically. Payment can be made in the same location as order placement. Multiple payment channels are available. Cash transfer is achieved in less than 3 days.	Fully integrated payment system automatically reconciles cash received to customer order. Cash transfer (guarantee) is instant.
S4.5 Returns management	There is a documented returns procedure that determines when and where product returns are accepted and how they are managed. Returned goods are clearly identified on receipt into the warehouse and their condition is checked to determine whether they can be returned to good stock. Defective goods are controlled such that they cannot unintentionally re-enter the supply chain.	All returns received are given a reason code to enable root cause analysis. There are options to maximise value of the returns to the business (including options to rework at client site, rework or sell through clearance).	Returns operations (collection, redelivery and rework disposal) are linked to Customer Relationship Management (CRM) systems to allow full cost to serve an account to be understood. Customer relationship and logistics processes include provision of actions to avoid returns if possible.

S5 Customer and channel segmentation

Customer and channel segmentation is the process by which the needs of different customers and channels are understood, and the supply chain is configured to serve each segment as required.

Description

In this process the needs of different customers and channels is understood, and the supply chain is configured to serve each segment as required.

Context

Increasingly there are multiple channels to market which require different capabilities. In addition, different customers demand very different services based on their sophistication, structure and scale. Satisfying these different, and potentially conflicting, needs in a cost effective manner requires careful planning.

Glossary

Activity Based Costing (ABC)

An approach that attributes costs to activities, objects and processes to support accurate product and process costing.

Demand

S5 Customer and channel segmentation

S5 Elements	Competency	Proficiency	Mastery
S5.1 Understanding needs and costs to serve	There are specific internal roles for different customer segments that provide some differentiation of offering. The cost to serve different customer segments is understood.	The cost to serve of different segments is understood using contribution level analysis.	There is a detailed understanding of the needs and profitability of each segment and sub-segment. The cost to serve of customer segments is analysed using activity-based costing methodologies for all direct and indirect costs.
S5.2 Service levels	Customers are offered a limited number of product/service options.	Customers are offered a level of supply chain service selected from a fixed, limited number of options. Customers are offered a standard product range with some tailoring to customer requirements.	The cost/profitability service trade-off is fully understood and used by both customers and the business. Large/high profit customers receive customised services (priced accordingly).
S5.3 Differentiated supply chains	Different customer segments are served via differentiated service options.	There are some different processes and/or facilities to serve different customers/channels according to their different needs. The RFP response includes pro formas (resources, productivity, cost) so that easy comparisons between competing bids can be made, and helps avoid contractor errors in data interpretation.	The supply chain is highly focused on delivering to different customer segments/channels and to different service levels. Specialised facilities and processes are used to optimise cost/service for each customer segment.

S6 New product development

Optimising the product range to balance customer needs and complexity including the development of new products.

Description
This profile considers the end-to-end supply chain, from supply of materials to final customer delivery.

Context
Unnecessary complexity is common in geographically dispersed organisations through different designs for similar or identical finished products; these are largely hidden costs. Successful new product development requires close integration across all functions.

Glossary
NPD

Abbreviation for New Product Development.

Demand

S6 New product development

S6 Elements	Competency	Proficiency	Mastery
S6.1 Process and governance	The methods the business uses to develop new product ideas and move them to 'actionable' ideas are clearly stated. There is an appropriate communication process in place for sharing major product or service developments. Launch dates and intermediate development milestones are defined for all new product programmes.	There is a clear strategy that sets objectives and allocates resources to achieve targets across 'continued product innovation' (incremental development) and 'discontinuous innovation' (breakthrough products). Potential, emerging and new technologies are all explicitly monitored to ensure all relevant innovation options are available for idea generation. A stage gate process is defined, which highlights progress towards stated launch dates, and drives remedial actions to be taken to enable successful launches. A detailed internal and external communication strategy is in place for major product or service developments.	The whole product pipeline from ideas to proto-products to 'close to launch' products is managed as a whole competitive proposition (rather than as isolated initiatives). Innovation of the whole service model is considered, not just the product. A stage gate process holds projects to their development time plans, or forces their rescheduling. Only in exceptional circumstances are projects allowed to continue if their launch dates are at risk.
S6.2 Range reviews	Product categories are defined, based mainly on market factors.	Ranges are reviewed at regular intervals according to a defined process. New Product Introductions (NPIs) and product retirements are planned based on the pareto of profitability/contribution as well as market considerations.	There is a senior level governance process to manage ranges reviews, with sign-off by Sales, Marketing and Supply Chain. The range management process balances total additional costs with forecast revenue.

(continued on next page)

S6 Elements

S6.3 Product design

Competency	Proficiency	Mastery
The product management process sets product standards to ensure that category and range management principles are adhered to. There has been some standardisation of specifications. Material costs are understood at product design stage and influence the specification. There are regular supplier forums for innovation and market analysis sharing.	There are guidelines in place to check that the product development process does not introduce unnecessary complexity. The RFP response includes pro formas (resources, productivity, cost) so that easy comparisons between competing bids can be made, and helps avoid contractor errors in data interpretation. Products are designed to optimise total manufacturing costs. The product management process ensures that products and specifications are standardised across different manufacturing locations. There is a recognised process for sharing, assessing and implementing supplier-initiated innovative proposals.	Additional complexity is only introduced where there is an overall benefit in the long term. All SKUs have standardised multi-purpose (e.g. multi-lingual) labelling and packaging (when regulations allow). Products are designed to simplify end-to-end supply chain management, including inventories and distribution. Processes are standardised to enable differentiation of the product at the latest stage in the production process. Key suppliers are involved from the beginning of the product design process. Suppliers are recognised at senior executive level as contributors to the competitive edge of the company and those that make the most difference are rewarded with more business, where appropriate.

S6.4 Product or service specification	A structure is in place to capture and communicate requirements. Specifications include functional requirements. Specifications are based on historic standards from similar existing items.	Cross-functional specification teams exist including procurement representation. Specification is value engineering based, maximising the value/cost ratio. Specifications are developed specially for the new product and signed off by all the cross-functional business stakeholders. Preferred suppliers are involved in setting specifications for the elements of a finished product which they supply.	Cross-functional specification teams are fully integrated into the organisation. There is a consistent approach to specifications, with clear technological direction and a clear understanding of market vs. requirements. Specifications are only signed off by all business stakeholders following successful trials.
S6.5 New product forecasts	New product forecasts are based on similar products and events. Launch volumes and first year volume forecasts are available prior to price estimation discussions with suppliers.	The regular evaluation of all NPI forecasts drives improvements in the forecasting process. Systems are designed to handle NPI through retaining historical event data. Launch volumes and first year volume forecasts are provided by markets prior to supplier selection.	A specific collaboration process is in place with trading partners on NPI forecasts. The NPI forecasts are expressed as a range of outcomes with implications and actions for each range extreme identified. Long range forecasts have been provided by markets prior to supplier contracting.
S6.6 Supplier selection	The Procurement team is consulted on New Product Development (NPD) and liaises with suppliers to provide prototypes and pricing. The Procurement team works with suppliers to advise on design specifications. Clear, unambiguous supplier evaluation criteria are generated.	The Procurement team is included in product development teams, recommending potential suppliers and providing cost and production ramp-up analysis. Technical trade-offs are reviewed as a team which includes procurement function, supplier and NPD. In-house and third party supply options have all been considered as part of the sourcing decision.	The Procurement team has a defined and fully integrated role in the NPD and NPI processes which includes a formal sign-off. Decisions are based on a combination of total cost management, target costing and activity based costing as appropriate.

(continued on next page)

S6 Elements	Competency	Proficiency	Mastery
S6.7 Obsolescence management	There is a documented process in place to manage material and finished good obsolescence as product designs change. Optimal phase out/phase in dates are set based on criticality/cost of change.	There is a focus on minimising obsolescence (including stock in the distribution network and at supplier locations) through a detailed, documented planning process for every product design change. All design changes costs include scrappage or have a stock run-out plan to minimise obsolescence costs.	The obsolescence plan is jointly owned with the suppliers who manage their own supply base impact. Obsolescence management is in a closed loop with stock rotation policy, inventory planning and other appropriate control techniques.

Demand

S7 Promotions planning

Sustainability in demand covers the ways in which the company seeks to inform or influence customer behaviour in support of its sustainability goals.

Description

This profile covers the ways in which the company seeks to inform or influence customer behaviour in support of its sustainability goals, as well as the extent to which markets perceive company activities as responsible in the context of sustainable development.

Context

Sustainability should extend through the whole lifecycle of the products; this profile is based on maximising sustainability after the products have been sold to customers and consumers.

S7 Elements	Competency	Proficiency	Mastery
S7.1 Policy and procedures	Documented promotions planning procedures are followed.	The documented promotions planning procedures define the roles and responsibilities throughout the promotions cycle.	Promotions planning procedures are continuously reviewed and improved.
S7.2 Trading partner communication	Suppliers are informed of changes to materials requirements that relate to one-off promotions.	There is close collaboration with suppliers on forecast volumes and dates. Contingency plans are shared with suppliers for sales above or below expectations.	Promotional calendars are shared with suppliers and other trading partners to enable capacity planning. There is daily planning during the promotional period, monitoring sales against targets and adjusting deployment plans as required. Promotional sales information is shared with relevant trading partners daily.
S7.3 Inventory planning	There is a detailed inventory planning process in place for promotions, based on ensuring sufficient launch quantities of the promotional product.	Inventory is held back centrally as much as is possible to enable quick response to local shortages. The RFP response includes pro formas (resources, productivity, cost) so that easy comparisons between competing bids can be made, and helps avoid contractor errors in data interpretation.	Promotional inventory planning is carried out collaboratively with all trading partners on a daily basis. Inventory deployment is based on different stock factors for each stock point based on expected uptake of the promotion.

Demand

S8 Sustainability in demand

Sustainability in demand covers the ways in which the company seeks to inform or influence customer behaviour in support of its sustainability goals.

Description

This profile covers the ways in which the company seeks to inform or influence customer behaviour in support of its sustainability goals, as well as the extent to which markets perceive company activities as responsible in the context of sustainable development.

Context

Sustainability should extend through the whole lifecycle of the products; this profile is based on maximising sustainability after the products have been sold to customers and consumers.

Glossary

Life Cycle Analysis

Analysis of the impact of a product throughout its lifecycle from raw materials supply, through manufacturing and distribution, and beyond the immediate customer to the final consumer, and beyond them to how it might be disposed of.

S8 Elements	Competency	Proficiency	Mastery
S8.1 Customer relationships and responsibility	Product labelling conforms to all current regional regulation and provides advice on recycling of product or packaging. The majority of packaging used is recyclable.	Product labelling provides contact details for advice or complaints. Packaging is fully recyclable or reusable.	Customers are encouraged (e.g. via website) to minimise or offset impacts of their own consumption. Promotional activity and delivery options are designed to minimise environmental and social impacts.
S8.2 Data, measurement and incentives	Clear and consistent guidelines exist to control packaging and labelling, with technical specialists to offer advice. Data is available on the packaging materials and quantities used per product.	Metrics are used to monitor returns volumes, customer complaints and packaging volumes consumed.	Life cycle analysis is used to minimise product and packaging waste throughout the supply chain. Staff are incentivised to achieve on-going reductions in product and packaging waste.

Foundation

- Intergrated working
- Education & training
- Data management and integrity
- KPI reporting
- Continual improvement
- Quality assurance
- Contingency management
- Sustainability strategy

7 Foundation

The Foundation processes cover areas which underpin all effective supply chains. Strong data management, reporting, education and training, and cross-functional working enable truly excellent processes. These need to be supported with robust processes for quality management, risk management and sustainability.

The Foundation processes are relevant across all supply chain functions, creating an environment in which it is possible to excel.

Integrated working covers cross-functional working and strategy communication throughout the organisation, ensuring that all of the staff are aligned to the same goals. Education and training covers the gathering and delivery of training requirements, ensuring that supply chain personnel are qualified to meet current and future business needs.

Accurate and timely data is a critical element of all operations. Supply chains are increasingly automated, with one or more computer system supporting and linking each function. The data management and integrity section covers data ownership, auditing and updating, ensuring that all data used within supply chain processes is suitably accurate and updated appropriately.

Effective management requires good reporting, to establish current performance and flag potential issues. Critically, targets and metrics should be integrated across the supply chain, encouraging the right behaviours to achieve common goals. This is covered in the KPI reporting section.

Continual improvement is the process of identifying, quantifying and prioritising all losses and developing a structured plan for elimination, sharing and reapplication. This fundamental activity applies to all areas of the supply chain and covers identifying improvements and executing them, from single-area instances to cross-functional teams, and reapplication of the enhancements to other areas or processes.

Quality assurance ensures quality is built into the design of all supply chain processes eliminating rework and defects. It is traditionally applied to manufacturing, but should apply to all areas of the supply chain. It covers quality assurance strategy, ownership and reporting, quality tools and skills used, and operating procedures and auditing.

Contingency management ensures there are policies and plans in place across the supply chain to deal with potential risks and disruptions. With the increasing reliance on global supply chains, it is critical that potential supply disruptions have contingency plans and risk mitigation including alternate sourcing, disaster recovery plans.

Sustainability strategy defines the supply chain approach that ensures best practice in the areas of environmental, ethical and social impact management. This section applies to senior management activity to direct policy and action planning throughout the supply chain, including resolution of conflicting priorities between long-term sustainability and short-term business pressures.

Foundation

F1 Integrated working

Integrated working ensures the business works in a co-ordinated and synchronised manner, with different functions communicating effectively to achieve common strategic and tactical objectives.

Description

This profile applies to all supply chain functions within a business unit, and tests how well integrated they are.

Context

Silo working, with limited communication between different functions, is a cause of sub-optimisation and errors. For an organisation to be effective there must be both alignment across the different functions and a common understanding of business direction and objectives irrespective of level within the organisation.

Foundation

F1 Integrated working

F1 Elements	Competency	Proficiency	Mastery
F1.1 Structure and business objectives	The organisational design has been documented and outlines regional and functional relationships and responsibilities. A supply chain strategy exists outlining key objectives.	The organisational design is linked to the supply chain strategy. Role descriptions have been developed detailing the key responsibilities and interdependencies by role.	Both cross-functional and line reporting structures are documented and aligned to relevant business processes such as Sales and Operations Planning (S&OP). The organisation design and role description detail is communicated and readily available to all employees.
F1.2 Communication	Formalised communication practices exist through the business. Cross-functional communication is centrally managed for the senior teams and department managers.	A central communication policy exists for all business announcements and is typically based on a monthly cycle. A variety of communication methods are used including face to face senior announcements, line management updates, and email and bulletin mediums. Formalised cross-functional communication is managed via standard business processes such as leadership meetings, S&OP and special projects.	The communication plan is actively managed and discussed with the senior team. The plan includes cross-business updates, road shows with senior representation and regular updates on business strategy and performance. The central communication policy is widely recognised and used by all levels of management. Communications are a combination of weekly, monthly and quarterly updates aligned to an overall communications strategy.

F1 Elements	Competency	Proficiency	Mastery
F1.3 Common language and shared metrics	Differences in regions and functions are recognised and documented. Examples include product family descriptions, compliance definitions and product lifecycle status. Senior management are aware of differences in terminology and adapt locally to suit local requirements (by business units or region).	Standard definitions are agreed for the business and communicated across all regions and functions. The RFP response includes pro formas (resources, productivity, cost) so that easy comparisons between competing bids can be made, and helps avoid contractor errors in data interpretation. A standard KPI dashboard is used for reporting purposes. Best practice terminology exists with clear documentation, definition and training across all regions and functions.	A global KPI dashboard exists and the same measures are used for reporting purposes and day to day management across all regions and functions. The KPI definitions include measure, description, proposed calculation, source data and explanation on how the information should be interpreted. Variations to standard are documented and included as part of the global master. Processes are standardised for all core/ strategic areas to facilitate best practice measurement and training.
F1.4 Business management processes	Business management processes have clear objectives with the right people involved. Business management meeting schedules are adhered to.	Regional/global/functional calendars are aligned and objectives are cross-referenced to ensure duplication is minimised.	Business management processes are aligned to the strategic objectives of the business. Meeting objectives, audience, agenda and accountabilities are clear with annual calendars established in advance.
F1.5 Training and education	All staff have been trained in basic supply chain principles including functional trade-offs, key performance metrics and core business processes.	Senior management is involved in cross-functional leadership meetings to challenge ways of working and discuss end-to-end optimisation challenges.	Business objectives are reviewed and aligned with improved ways of working and end-to-end opportunities driven through cross-functional challenges. Thought leadership programmes exist to encourage cross-functional thinking and improvement.

Foundation

Education and training processes ensure supply chain personnel are educated and trained to meet current and future business needs.

Description

Education and training applies to the organisation as a whole and covers the development of requirements, how they are transformed into training plans, how training material is developed and how qualification can be tracked against it.

Context

Education and training requirements, and resulting training plans, should be driven by the business plan requirements and results analysis relating to all supply chain processes.

Foundation

F2 Education and training

F2 Elements	Competency	Proficiency	Mastery
F2.1 Development planning	A framework of skills and competencies by role and function exists. The framework links to an individual's personal development plan/annual appraisal or a functional need. All training and education requirements are documented and aligned to the business needs. Training plans are in place for each department.	As part of the business strategy, an education and training plan is developed across the business and built into individual objectives. A training schedule is in place for at least the next 3-6 month period to address the needs of the individuals/teams. The progress of training and education is fully documented and audited to ensure that the training plan is delivering the business needs.	A robust process is in place to ensure effective training is being provided to meet current and future business needs. Programmes are devised to develop 'T-shaped' management (technical depth in functional area with wide business appreciation). Modules are prioritised, delivered and measured for success. The schedule covers at least 12 months by department/function.
F2.2 Education and training requirements	Formal individual training plans are linked to a management review process.	Individual core competencies are identified through the staff assessment process. There is a process for follow-up refresher courses where necessary within an agreed period of time.	A balance of both internal and external training courses are used to match the business and individual needs across local, regional or global perspectives. Training modules are created and delivered against an appropriate time plan and budget. Recognised qualifications form part of a specific skill set. Any internal qualification recognised by the global corporation is followed up by a robust programme of control which ensures the learning is still relevant.

F2 Elements	Competency	Proficiency	Mastery
F2.3 Training material	In-house standard vocational training programmes and 'on the job training' are available for staff with supporting information.	In-house training programmes and 'on the job training' are complemented by the use of intranet and web based education methods. The RFP response includes pro formas (resources, productivity, cost) so that easy comparisons between competing bids can be made, and helps avoid contractor errors in data interpretation. Training allows cross-functional and cross-regional sharing and learning.	Training material is consistently developed in line with the training strategy. Flagship events are delivered through an on-site university/academy or shared education facility, including appropriate externally delivered content. There is an active use of regional/global management training initiatives and skills transfer.
F2.4 Training methods	Specific trainers or 'on the job experts' are used with a small budget allocated for supporting materials. A balanced use of internal and external management training courses exists to match business needs.	Non vocational staff education programmes supplement specific vocational training. External/internal facilitator led training is used to deliver more specialist areas/topics or larger groups where team interaction is necessary. Budget is allocated to each module based upon a prioritised plan.	The external/internal facilitator led training plan is refreshed every 12 months.

F2.5 Process and performance measurement	There are defined processes for training and development that are periodically reviewed. Performance is reviewed as part of the individual's annual appraisal.	Structured assessment programmes are in place and reviewed annually. Departmental/line managers and training coordinators own and develop relevant training plans.	Self-development initiatives are actively encouraged. An established employee appraisal process is followed and linked to personal objectives and development plans. Training material is reviewed annually for relevance. Heads of department, training coordinators and HR manage the training material and programme, refreshing as necessary for topical and relevant subject matter.
F2.6 Reporting	Reporting is done quarterly and tracks who, what, when and spend for the training conducted in that period.	A specific measure and target is outlined for a monthly report and submitted to heads of department to track against budget.	Robust measurement of month-on-month training is tracked against a framework of skills and competencies. The relevant outputs are measured to show the impact of training investment.

Data management and integrity ensures that all data used within supply chain processes is suitably accurate and updated appropriately.

Description

This profile covers data management and integration of systems across the business. There is a focus on the areas which impact supply chain operations - item master data, the flow of data from forecasts through the planning systems, and orders.

Context

Effective data management is critical to efficient supply chain operations: poor data leads to errors, possible service level failures and lower efficiency.

Glossary

Cycle counting

Process by which stock levels are continually monitored negating the requirement for a periodic total stock take. Frequency of count and accuracy tolerance are set by SKU or category as appropriate to their criticality and value.

Gap analysis

Reviewing results versus a pre-assigned target, often completing pareto analysis to highlight the biggest issues.

Foundation

F3 Data management and integrity

F3 Elements	Competency	Proficiency	Mastery
F3.1 Ownership	There is a single entry for each set of data, with no duplications, which is readily accessible to those who need it. There are clear guidelines for the responsibility of initial data entry, maintaining and updating data records. Data management security is defined within applications.	There is clear ownership and accountability at a local level for specific data records; those responsible understand how the data is used. Data management security is defined at field level within applications.	Those responsible understand the importance of accuracy and timely data creation and maintenance. Data and information governance is centralised wherever possible. Data ownership between operations and sales organisations is clear. Data quality standards are defined and understood and data has been standardised.
F3.2 Audit processes	There are audits of accuracy across all data records. There are system audit trails that identify who amended data and on what date. A system health audit has been completed within the last year and resulting actions followed through.	The data management process guarantees that each piece of data is updated at the right time by the right people to support process execution. Audit procedures are used at least monthly and are statistically sound (e.g. cycle counting for inventory). A system health audit is completed at least quarterly with resulting actions monitored until resolved or escalated as appropriate.	There are clear processes and governance for data management to ensure its accuracy and timeliness of update. The data management process covers procedures for changes, additions and deletions of master data information and all the static data elements are reviewed at least yearly. A system health audit is completed monthly, with a monthly action plan driven by the gap analysis.

(continued on next page)

F3 Elements	Competency	Proficiency	Mastery
F3.3 Data transfer	There are checks to guarantee that any manually entered data matches the original.	Data transfers occur through system to system integration. The RFP response includes pro formas (resources, productivity, cost) so that easy comparisons between competing bids can be made, and helps avoid contractor errors in data interpretation.	There is no manual entry of data anywhere in the organisation. All operational planning data is held on a single integrated system rather than on spreadsheets. Spreadsheets are only used for one off simulations/'what-if' analysis. Data is transferred from system to system through integrated routines.
F3.4 Data	Information is available and structured in fixed formats. Data can be easily located by non-expert users.	Data required from internal and external sources is defined and captured accurately. Information is available in meaningful formats and is accessed as needed. One single set of data is used throughout the business.	Information is gathered at source and available on request to all authorised staff to enable them to do their jobs. Consistent data is available to all business users as required.
F3.5 Reporting systems	Formal reporting systems are used to generate information required.	A user-friendly interface enables all staff to create ad hoc reports as required. An intranet holds companywide standards, best practice and contact information.	A sophisticated online executive information system is available and used extensively for all reporting requirements.

F4 KPI reporting

KPI reporting ensures performance data is communicated in the appropriate format and required frequency to support operations and improvement.

Description
This profile applies across the whole supply chain and covers scope and standardisation of performance measures, reporting systems and targets, and reporting mechanisms and formats.

Context
To enable effective review of supply chain processes, performance data must be available to those managing the processes to aid effective decision making and improvement activities. KPIs alone drive little without standardisation, target setting and review.

Glossary
Dashboard/Scorecard
Visual method of displaying KPIs against their targets e.g. green for on target, red for off target.

KPI reporting ensures performance data is communicated in the appropriate format and required frequency to support operations and improvement.

Balanced Scorecard
A structured measurement system based on a mix of financial and non-financial measures of business performance.

CSFs
Abbreviation for Critical Success Factors - those activities and processes that must be done to enable the company to reach its goals.

Gap analysis
Reviewing results versus a pre-assigned target, often completing pareto analysis to highlight the biggest issues.

Foundation

F4 KPI reporting

F4 Elements	Competency	Proficiency	Mastery
F4.1 Scope of performance measures	Each function, department or work team measures the internal performance of its own processes. There is a companywide view of performance.	A balanced scorecard of market, process and financial measures is used to inform decisions and track performance.	Improvement targets and plans are in place to support each measure.
F4.2 Standardisation	Performance measures have definitions.	All performance measures and definitions are standardised.	All performance reports have standardised timing and formats, and are consolidated regionally/globally and regularly produced.
F4.3 Information systems	Online information is updated daily, directly from business intelligence systems.	Trend and history information is available with 'what if' modelling capability. The RFP response includes pro formas (resources, productivity, cost) so that easy comparisons between competing bids can be made, and helps avoid contractor errors in data interpretation. The use of dashboards and scorecards is common.	Dashboards and scorecards are established as routine ways of monitoring business performance. Auto alert mechanisms are in place.
F4.4 Targets	Standardised, globally/regionally coordinated targets are in place.	Targets are driven by and integrated with company strategy.	Targets are integrated with the objectives/bonus structures of employees. There is a mix of short-term and medium-term targets to drive a balanced outcome.

Continual improvement is the process of identifying, quantifying and prioritising all losses and developing a structured plan for elimination, sharing and reapplication.

Description

This profile applies to all areas across the supply chain and covers identifying and executing improvements from single improvements to cross-functional improvement teams, and reapplication of improvements to other areas/processes that will benefit.

Context

Continual improvement increases performance across the supply chain. This profile sets out a business wide framework for managing improvements across all functions.

Glossary

Gap analysis

Reviewing results versus a pre-assigned target, often completing pareto analysis to highlight the biggest issues.

Zero-based loss analysis

Reviewing results versus a zero-loss base (what is the total loss rather than just against the target). For example, waste of a certain material might be below target % but the highest in terms of value and hence, should be a priority.

Reapplication

The process of assessing whether a particular improvement is applicable to other areas or processes and ensuring the improvements are then shared and implemented to ensure benefits and/or standardisation are achieved.

Quality tools

The quality improvement tools such as why-why, fishbone/cause & effect, pareto and control charts.

Single Improvements (Kaizens)

A single implemented improvement. Normally a kaizen refers to the one-page summary sheet which is used for sharing, re-applying and recognising improvements. Usually has the following sections: before and after (photo/diagram), what work was done, what results were achieved including quantifiable savings if possible and potential reapplication opportunities.

Charters

A statement summarising the objectives and scope of an improvement team. This should cover who is involved, what the objectives/targets are, what is the scope, timings etc. The statement is very useful for summarising the work and for approving the work, making it visible to all and for assessing progress. Often seen on an activity board (see above).

F5 Elements	Competency	Proficiency	Mastery
F5.1 Business philosophy	Continuous improvement is understood by top management and reviewed as part of the annual business planning processes. Targets are cascaded down the organisation and linked to budgets.	Continuous improvement is reviewed as part of a cross-functional improvement process. A project management approach is applied for large scale initiatives. The policy is signed off at a business unit level.	Continuous improvement is recognised as a fundamental business principle and actively practised across all levels of the organisation. A formalised top-down approach uses zero loss analysis and bottom-up input from employee innovations to identify losses and opportunities across all areas of the business. Small 'Kaizen' type improvements are incorporated into cross-business/region process reengineering with all improvement linked to business needs.
F5.2 Improvement teams	Functional owners are assigned to lead improvement activities within their area and are responsible for resourcing and delivery. Additional functional areas are involved upon request from the functional leader.	Improvement teams are established to lead improvement activities, responsible for eliminating specific losses. Formal charters listing objectives, timescales, resources, responsibilities and expected results are completed for the top initiatives.	Formalised improvement teams are in place with cross-functional representation at all levels. Team structure is linked to a cross-area/regional reporting hierarchy for reporting and reapplication purposes. Specialist loss elimination teams are established for the high priority areas. A self-managed team structure is used to manage next level priorities.

F5.3 Zero-based loss analysis and calculation	Functional driven analysis is in place with losses defined as the gap between current performance and target performance. Measures include % variance to targets.	Target performance is based upon 'zero-base' but may be limited to the visible opportunity (e.g. line speed, quality performance). The RFP response includes pro formas (resources, productivity, cost) so that easy comparisons between competing bids can be made, and helps avoid contractor errors in data interpretation.	Target performance (zero-based) is unconstrained by experience, culture, cost accounting and KPI targets. Losses are reviewed simultaneously across all areas - transport, warehousing, manufacturing, procurement, administration and support, and planning. All opportunities are converted to value for comparative purposes and criteria are used to assess the priority by value and the alignment to company goals.
F5.4 Tools	Basic brainstorming and validation processes are used to assess opportunities. Root cause analysis tools are used.	Root cause analysis tools are used in a structured way. Examples include why-why, cause and effect, 6 sigma, lean toolbox and advanced troubleshooting.	The business has selected a preferred toolbox and applies it consistently across all levels to simulate the root cause and corrective actions.
F5.5 Reporting	Loss eliminating activities are documented. Performance against targets is reported within departments.	Activities are documented formally in an action plan identifying loss opportunity, current and target performance, actions to resolve with clear accountabilities. There is a time phased implementation plan for loss reduction which is monitored. Progress against targets is discussed on a monthly basis with senior teams.	All activities are included in an overall improvement plan visible to all stakeholders and linked to business values, departments and individual objectives. Cross-functional and regional plans link into an overall target. Progress versus target is reported and made visible to all employees on a monthly basis. Team charters, action plans and detailed loss analysis is easily accessible for all stakeholders.
F5.6 Re-application	A re-application process is in place with standard templates for sharing and implementation in other applicable areas.	Local reapplication processes include visual displays of improvements and a database for sharing and control purposes.	A policy governs reapplication and ensures improvements are validated and rolled out to similar processes across the regional/ global business units as applicable.

Foundation

F6 Quality assurance

Quality assurance ensures quality is built into the design of all supply chain processes, eliminating rework and defects.

Description

This profile applies to all areas of the supply chain and covers quality assurance strategy, ownership, reporting, quality tools, skills used, operating procedures and auditing. Supplier quality assurance is covered in more detail in the Buy profiles.

Context

Without effective quality assurance, defects can exist within products, services and processes potentially leading to loss of revenue and costly inspection, rework or waste.

Glossary

SPC

Statistical Process Control (SPC) is the method of using statistical tools to observe process behaviour and make decisions based upon this data. A popular form is a control chart with upper and lower limits where data points are plotted to observe if the process is in control.

Gap analysis

Reviewing results versus a pre-assigned target, often completing pareto analysis to highlight the biggest issues.

CoA

Abbreviation for a Certificate of Analysis, a confirmation that product conforms to attribute and analytical quality requirements sent to the customer to negate need for incoming inspection.

Self-assessments

Process where the people responsible for an area or process assess themselves against pre or self-determined criteria to look for potential failures before they happen or are picked up on an external audit.

F6 Elements	Competency	Proficiency	Mastery
F6.1 Strategy	There is a quality assurance programme by functional area. A quality strategy exists covering the prevention of customer/consumer defects.	There is an integrated quality assurance programme across the supply chain including suppliers. The quality strategy also covers the elimination of non-value adding rework, inspection and waste. A Statistical Process Control (SPC) approach is the foundation with process capability defined and measured for all key attributes.	There is a fully integrated SPC programme embedded across the full supply chain. The quality assurance strategy is focused on preventing all defects across products and processes with continuous improvement plans in place.
F6.2 Ownership	There is shared responsibility for quality assurance between operations and the quality function.	Quality assurance is seen as an integral part of operational processes and teams. Quality assurance is considered a joint responsibility with joint problem solving.	Quality assurance is part of daily work with the quality function providing the centre of expertise where required.
F6.3 Performance monitoring	Quality results are reported monthly by function and customised reports are sent to customers and suppliers. Quality gap analysis occurs monthly covering defects and customer complaints. Quality issues are identified for root cause and preventative actions put in place.	Quality results reported cover the total supply chain. Quality gap analysis also covers quality process failures. Cross-functional teams work on quality improvement with input from suppliers and customers as required.	Quality is included in regular bottom-up loss analysis. Root causes at a system level (e.g. training or documentation) are analysed for common themes and mitigating actions are put in place. Suppliers and customers are embedded into the quality improvement process.

F6.4 Release criteria	A Certificate of Analysis (CoA) is used to release the product to the customer. Online Quality Control (QC) sampling is in place.	The QC and SPC data is shared. Regular quality assurance audits are carried out by the customer.	The SPC approach is fully implemented online. There is a joint approach to Quality Assurance (QA) between customer and supplier. Yearly auditing from customers is in place to validate finished goods quality assurance.
F6.5 Documentation control	All processes are formally documented. Methods of change control are in place.	All processes are formally controlled with identified ownership. A formal mechanism is in place for improving operating procedures and updating documentation.	All critical information concerning parameters and control conditions is included in documentation. A formal system is embedded which complements the continuous improvement process and facilitates rapid, effective implementation of improvements and updating supporting documentation.
F6.6 Audits	The Quality function carries out audits of the quality assurance processes across the supply chain at least every year to identify improvement areas.	Results and the integrated improvement plan are owned by the central Quality function. Structured self-improvement assessments are in place.	Quality self-improvement is a formal programme and teams carry out self-assessments for weaknesses in people and processes. The self-assessments are completed annually and the likelihood and potential impact of a failure are used to determine priorities.

Foundation

F7 Contingency management

Contingency management ensures there are policies and plans in place across the supply chain to deal with potential risks and disruptions.

Description

The profile applies to the entire supply chain from suppliers through to production sites, the logistics network and third-party distributors.

Context

With the increasing reliance on global supply chains, it is critical that potential supply disruptions have contingency plans and risk mitigation including alternate sourcing, disaster recovery plans.

Glossary

SLA

Abbreviation for a Service Level Agreement, an agreement between the supplying and receiving parties defining how the service is provided. At its most basic, an SLA details service and quality levels, but can cover every aspect of supply from cost, delivery, returns, innovation and improvement.

Foundation

F7 Contingency management

F7 Elements	Competency	Proficiency	Mastery
F7.1 Policy	There is a documented contingency planning policy in place with required plans and responsibilities for all supply chain functions.	Contingency plans have been communicated to all relevant key employees. Contingency plans have been agreed and shared with key trading partners as necessary including suppliers, logistics providers and distributors. All documentation on contingency planning are stored on a central database.	Contingency plans are tested at least annually to ensure that plans are effective, well understood, and the required capabilities are in place.
F7.2 Contingency planning	There are annual reviews of contingency plans which understand the risks, both direct and indirect, to the business from operational issues. Each business functions are analysed to determine potential risks, both direct and indirect, along with the impact and probability of each.	Critical trading partners (suppliers, logistics providers and distributors) are involved in risk reviews and in developing contingency plans. Reviews are based on detailed company and external industry data on all potential risks to supply. There is an annual process in place whereby the sales and marketing team reviews priority customers and propose changes to the priority customers list.	Contingency planning strategy evolves and re-evaluates the cost to the business of production and supply failure over time.

(continued on next page)

F7 Elements

F7.3 Contingency sourcing plans

Competency	Proficiency	Mastery
Contingency sourcing plans for a total loss of the factory have been developed for the priority products (inclusive of those products manufactured at third party manufacturers). The Service Level Agreements (SLAs) include guaranteed volume by product and end market, duration of supply, lead (response) time for first supply from alternative source, product acceptance of any trade-offs, any legal implications.	Contingency supply solutions are identified when sourcing changes are proposed. The RFP response includes pro formas (resources, productivity, cost) so that easy comparisons between competing bids can be made, and helps avoid contractor errors in data interpretation. Contingency sourcing plans have been developed for different disaster scenarios. The SLAs include any responsibilities by parties to maintain agreed state of readiness, and if applicable the SLA should specify which lower priority products need to be dropped to manufacture the priority products in a contingency event. There is visibility of a regularly updated priority products list.	Contingency sourcing plans have been developed for different disaster scenarios. Contingency distribution plans have been developed for different disaster scenarios. There is an annual process in place whereby the sales and marketing teams review priority customers and propose changes to the priority customers list.

F7.4 Supplier risk management	Supply risk management is focused on supplier's financial viability and ability to deal with global catastrophic events.	Supply risk management includes factors such as inbound logistics, contingency planning, currency and commodity fluctuation and demand spikes. Supplier disaster recovery plans are included in all tenders. Tier 1 suppliers are categorised into strategy groups based on their performance in managing risk and their risk environment.	Tier 1 and 2 suppliers are categorised into strategy groups based on their performance in managing risk and their risk environment. Potential risks are identified for each strategy groups and mitigation strategies are in place for each group.
F7.5 Business continuity planning	There is a crisis management team empowered to control any interruptions of the business. The consequences of an outage of service is analysed in quantifiable financial terms, operational impacts, and legal or regulatory restrictions.	A recovery time frame exists for each business function which defines the point at which consequences of an outage are unacceptable. Recovery alternatives that cost effectively restore critical business functions within an acceptable time frame are identified.	A recovery plan is developed around the recovery solution authorised by management.

Foundation

F8 Sustainability strategy

Sustainability strategy defines the supply chain approach to ensure application of best practice in the areas of environmental, ethical and social impact management.

Description

This profile applies to senior management activity to direct policy and action planning throughout the supply chain, including resolution of conflicting priorities between long-term sustainability and short-term business pressures. It covers policy setting across multiple sites or territories and the coordination of complex sustainability initiatives across the whole supply chain activity within the company.

Context

Sustainability issues can quickly enter the public domain, with potentially devastating effects to company reputation and operations. It is vital that environmental, ethical and social issues are handled in a coordinated, consistent and professional manner in order to minimise the risk of disruption to the supply chain. By its nature, supply chain sustainability strategy links all of the other processes in the supply chain, by setting policies and standards against which operations and plans should be assessed. In the Foundation layer, it should also have strong links to education and training, to build awareness and competency in managing complex issues.

Foundation

F8 Sustainability strategy

F8 Elements	Competency	Proficiency	Mastery
F8.1 Sustainability strategy and policy	The company has a clear and communicated set of principles governing management of environmental, ethical and social issues across all its supply chain activities.	The Board and delegated senior managers set and monitor appropriate policies to govern specific issues (e.g. ethical treatment of suppliers and sub-contractors).	The company employs external auditors to monitor and report on the execution of company activities in relation to the sustainability strategy and policies.
F8.2 Data, measurement and incentives	The sustainability strategy is translated into meaningful action plans and backed up by credible data and metrics.	The metrics hierarchy links site reporting through territories to global reporting. Performance is reviewed by the main Board and progress is published to shareholders and other stakeholders in an appropriate form.	Sound management of sustainability issues is linked to staff review and reward mechanisms at all levels. Sustainability is identified as a mandatory competency for all staff employed in senior supply chain management roles.

8 Frequently Asked Questions (FAQs)

Why should I benchmark?

When used properly, benchmarking provides insight through comparison of different business units, sites or organisations. For example, working capital levels might be compared with other companies in the same sector, which can then be used to prompt an examination of performance and processes.

Why should I use process as opposed to quantitative benchmarking?

'Process' benchmarking tends to have a deeper impact since robust, effective processes are the building blocks of a profitable and competitive organisation. Measuring process excellence against a standard can give an accurate view of capability in each part of a business. However, the first challenge is always to select the right standard, recognising that the most appropriate comparison might differ for each business area. The essential element in selecting the standards, or targets, is understanding what drives competitive advantage for the business.

What are the benefits of sc*prime*®?

sc**prime**® drives a focused and effective improvement programme, hard-wired to strategy and objectives. It has been proven to achieve a step-change in performance, with long term improvements already seen in over 20 countries on five continents, through aligning supply chain strategy to business strategy. Operating cost can be reduced by 15 – 20% and working capital lowered by 30 – 40% Further supply chain benefits are outlined on page 11.

Why should I use the sc*prime*® benchmarking approach?

Anybody who wants to improve, align, or standardise their supply chain can use the sc**prime**® approach. Specific areas of application are:

- Driving through a change programme; the examples we have seen are in moving from country-based business units to integrated regional and global operations organisations

- As part of major IT implementations, as a pre-implementation wave to assess process robustness and to drive improvement and standardisation. Inconsistencies can then be ironed out before the system is implemented. As an example, in a recent APO implementation the approach was used to define the minimum levels of process maturity and the required improvement actions. This ensured that the next wave of benefits could be delivered from the use of sophisticated optimisation tools

- Integrating mergers and acquisitions by aligning processes. How does the acquisition align with processes within the acquirer? What needs to be done to align them? What are the strengths and weaknesses of each organisation? Strengths can be taken as the new standards

- To drive longer term continuous improvement, becoming part of the culture and raising the standards of operations globally. The critical aspect is that it allows alignment with business strategy, rather than simply being based on industry best practice or cost reduction

How is sc*prime*® different to other benchmarking approaches, such as SCOR?
SCOR provides standard descriptions of management processes and metrics. Such definitions are useful but do not provide a mechanism for evaluating process maturity, or help define the needed improvement actions. sc**prime**® not only identifies best practice but also clearly defines the steps in the improvement journey.

How much time will it take and what type of resources will we need?
Setting up a new sc**prime**® programme, with a full end-to-end supply chain scope, will typically take 3-4 months from initiation to full operation. Programmes with narrower scope will be quicker. The development phase requires input from 'subject matter experts' from each function in the business, to support development of the customised process 'profiles'. The operational phase requires 'assessors'; they should have expertise in each functional area, and also have good interviewing and communication skills. Making the improvements will draw on a wide variety of skill sets in each business.

How does it work in practice?
Once the toolkit has been customised for the organisation, the approach is based on the 'improvement cycle'. A team will visit a site and carry out an assessment. Part of the philosophy of sc**prime**® is that this team should be wholly client-staffed, rather than consultant-staffed, as early as possible.

Based on the results, an improvement action plan is developed and agreed. The improvements are actioned, potentially with a combination of local, regional and/or global resources as appropriate. The assessment cycle ensures that a team will revisit the site, typically within 18 months, to ensure that higher process standards have been maintained.

Who am I being compared to in my benchmark reports?

Effective process benchmarking needs some level of customised process standards. The standard, or benchmark, is then based on each company's strategy, sector and particular needs. There must be a close fit with the company's specific business objectives and needs, a focus on the improvement path, and the business must believe the benchmarks and 'own' the results.

The essential element in selecting the standards or targets is understanding what drives competitive advantage for the business. At what does a business merely have to do 'well' and at what must it excel? Just doing 'well' might mean targeting best practice in that sector, but for the areas where competitive advantage is sought, a wider sector view is needed. The key is to focus on what the business wants to achieve.

What do I receive?

sc**prime**® contains supply chain-wide process benchmarks which are modular and customisable, and in 'roadmap' format, showing the paths to excellence. It also contains other elements, part of an overall 'toolkit', which can be packaged into a complete solution to drive improvement in the short, medium and long term.

Crimson & Co has worked alongside many multinational and local organisations to support the development and initial operation of an sc**prime**® programme. We work in conjunction with our clients' teams to develop the right programme for their organisations, focusing on their prioritised business needs and goals to create a sustainable and effective continuous improvement methodology.

We have multiple supply chains. Should we benchmark each individually or simply submit one survey that captures data for all areas of the company in a rolled-up fashion?

We suggest measuring each supply chain, or business unit, separately, and comparing each of them to a business's own standards. This will enable the business to identify and action weaknesses, and share strengths.

What metrics will be used?

sc**prime**® is based on benchmarking processes against a standard. The key metrics delivered through the toolkit measure achievement against the standards, for each business unit by process area. These metrics drive the improvement programme. Tracking normal 'quantitative' business metrics should continue, to measure benefits and progress to target levels of performance.

People capabilities

Introduction

People are often described as a business's greatest asset, and it is certainly true that in order to turn strategy into reality, a business needs effective people.

Despite this, how much do businesses really know about the capabilities that exist across their teams? To what extent are their existing capabilities constraining performance? How much more could be achieved by increasing these capabilities?

The sc**prime**® capability framework is designed to answer these questions and drive corrective action. It clearly defines the capabilities needed to deliver the full range of supply chain processes and is applicable to a wide range of businesses.

Whether an organisation's plans are focused on growth, rationalisation, acquisition, integration or just simply improving business as usual, the framework identifies whether the existing team has the capability to deliver those plans, and, if not, where the gaps are.

Most businesses use job descriptions, and increasingly they now have more detailed role profiles. In the majority of cases the key focus is to drive improved clarity and consistency across their teams.

The sc**prime**® capability profiles go further than this; they don't describe what a person needs to do, rather they identify the skills and capabilities required to do it. When tailored to an individual business, they provide a clear set of needs specifically linked to the business strategy.

If effective people are the key to turning strategy into reality, then building development plans for those people directly from the business plans is a huge step towards making this happen.

9 What is the scprime® people capability framework?

The sc**prime**® people capability framework is based around a set of profiles which describe the specific capabilities required to deliver best practice within each functional area across the supply chain.

The framework covers the end-to-end supply chain organisation structure, across the BUY, MAKE, PLAN, DELIVER and DEMAND functions. There are several people capability profiles within each functional area; the full framework of profiles is shown in Figure 1. on the next page. The FOUNDATION profiles cover core disciplines applicable across the different supply chain functions.

As with the sc**prime**® process capabilities, this is a modular system allowing businesses to select appropriate sections for their specific needs. Although built on the same knowledge base as the sc**prime**® process capabilities, the framework can be used as a stand-alone tool.

The people capability definitions are at a detailed level and reflect regularly-updated best practice based on real experience, and are ready to be adapted to a business's language, structure and ways of working. They allow a thorough and objective assessment of people capabilities across operations, regionally or globally.

Figure 1

People capabilities

Buy	Make	Plan
Sourcing and category management	Scheduling approach and delivery	S&OP
Supplier management and development	Asset management and maintenance	Finished goods inventory management
Operational purchasing	Production systems	Supply management
Materials management and planning	High performing teams	New product introduction

Deliver	Demand	Foundation
Network design and management	Demand management	Direction, policy and management
Warehouse management	Customer and channel management	Integrated supply chain
Transport management	Sales order cycle management	Change management
Contractor management	Category and range management	Process management
		Financial acumen
		Risk management
		Quality management
		Continuous improvement
		Project management

Each sc**prime**® people capability profile describes capabilities across three common areas:

Knowledge: what degree of previous knowledge and experience does the role holder need to be effective in delivering within this discipline?

Application: what capabilities are expected if the role holder is to use their knowledge to manage effective systems and processes in this area?

Control: what are the expectations for the role holder to control the process, including the effective control of data, exceptions, and process refinement?

For each of these areas there are three levels of capability:

- **Understands:** knows what the discipline involves, the general principles, foundations and critical get rights. Knows the terminology used and the common KPIs. Is aware of recent history such as issues and approach. Must be able to discuss and input into a meeting on this subject and support decision-making

- **Executes:** understands the area in detail and is able to operate the tasks with minimal support, including diagnosis and resolving daily issues. Has a good knowledge of different approaches and their relevant strengths. Is aware of what good looks like across all key performance indicators. Must have a track record of effective delivery in this area, including control and improvement in processes and metrics

- **Transforms:** able to shape the operating performance of the process, including step change improvements. Has experienced different approaches in this area and can benchmark performance. Has the drive to be able to influence and establish new approaches in terms of teams, reporting lines and measurement. Must possess a range of ideas and solutions, and be able to reapply these and show a track record of step change metric improvement

These different levels enable the profiles to be applied to a wide range of individuals; from those shaping and setting strategy, to those directly involved in delivering a process, to those who just need sufficient knowledge to complete their own role effectively.

Example people capability profiles for each function are shown on the following pages.

The full framework comprises similar profiles for each capability area in Figure 1. Each role is likely to need capabilities from a number of areas from the overall framework, covering the main functional area, adjacent functional areas and some Foundation capabilities.

As well as helping to better define the capabilities needed for each role, the detail within the profiles ensures that any gaps that are found are very clear, enabling the resulting development actions to be specific and more likely to succeed.

The people capability profiles are at the core of the overall framework. However, there are other components required to create an overall improvement toolkit:

- Training and education material, to be used to close capability gaps. Crimson & Co has a wide range of material covering the end-to-end supply chain

- A training course for assessors, to ensure high quality assessments. This should cover general questioning and assessment skills and techniques as well as the specific functional content

BC1 Sourcing and category management

Example profile

	1 - Understands	2 - Executes	3 - Transforms
Knowledge	Can explain the theory behind splitting products and services into categories, and is aware of the categories that exist in the organisation. Can give examples of how these categories behave and some key differences between them. Can clearly describe key stakeholders and where they sit on the stakeholder map (from champion to blocker). Explains how the strategic sourcing process works and how it balances procurement requirements including price.	Demonstrates knowledge of the structure of categories within the organisation, and uses knowledge of each to maintain alignment and exploit synergies. Leverage expertise and ensure team structure. Risk assessed to avoid one person holding all the influence. Selects the most appropriate tool for a category and ensures its use is optimised. Understands what is required from stakeholder involvement; can identify key people and actions to drive and how to maximise their impact. Has experience of different negotiation techniques and their application. Can extract information from existing data sources to build a clear case for stakeholders. Has experience of historical market performance and future predicted events/ trends to ensure they are reflected in category strategy.	Has wide-ranging experience of how to structure new categories (or restructure existing) in scenarios such as New Product Introduction (NPI), major market changes, or business development - and flex based upon market conditions. Can accurately define current drivers/levers and market conditions at category level. Has experience of aligning stakeholder plans to business strategy, and can develop links within an industry to shape future developments in line with business plans. Has experience in different category approaches (including when not to divide into categories at all) and the relative merits of each. Can compare current systems to these others. Is aware of what best practice in category management looks like and how the approaches of direct competitors differs from their own. Shapes/leads market thinking and is involved in relevant trade bodies. Trains and coaches others in strategic sourcing and category management.

Application			
	Understands the tools applied by the business, the standard approach and their own involvement in it. Can articulate the importance of specifications and accurate demand forecast. Understands the differing requirements of those involved in the category management process.	Can write a RFx that accurately reflects/ describes the key requirements being placed on suppliers through understanding what elements need to be included, and ensuring the right stakeholders are consulted to provide this information. Can negotiate with suppliers regarding the outputs of the process. Able to model the current situation through spend analysis, demand review and market to define a category management approach and sourcing strategy. Is able to present data tailored to different stakeholder groups/needs as part of driving alignment and buy in, identifying new sourcing opportunities where appropriate. Has set review cycles that are specific to the needs of each category and can explain this based upon factors such as volatility, seasonality, historic trends. Demonstrates faster process change and decision making as a result of tailored review frequencies. Maximises contract knowledge through leveraging mechanisms such as price breaks.	Ensures that the principles underpinning the strategic sourcing and category management approach are embedded within the business and updated when required. Shows innovation in the use of strategic sourcing and category management tools and is able to challenge the use of, or move to, buying organisations in delivering a step change in the delivery of the sourcing function. Can gather intelligence from internal and external sources to give direction on future requirements.

BC1 Sourcing and category management

Example profile

Control

1 - Understands	2 - Executes	3 - Transforms
Is aware of the KPIs that are used in tracking the delivery/achievement of the strategic sourcing and category management process over time, and the current level of performance against these. Able to gauge stakeholder involvement within own area, and understands how to increase engagement and participation where required.	Uses judgement in determining when working outside of standard processes is the correct approach, and can develop appropriate temporary controls in these situations (e.g. needing to move quickly to maintain supply when a supplier has gone bust). From experience, has completed a risk/impact assessment for each category and implements appropriate controls to mitigate these (such as specific contract terms, or supplier duplication). Able to stand back and identify where there are gaps in knowledge (market, suppliers, usage) that limit the sourcing effectiveness and can identify ways of closing these gaps. Runs effective post-implementation reviews that not only rectify on-going gaps in delivery, but also identify areas to be improved in future supplier selection and contract term definition. Has set appropriate KPIs and targets by category to drive behaviours based upon knowledge of current performance and future market conditions. Structures contracts with appropriate Service Level Agreements (SLAs) to ensure good supplier performance throughout the life of the contract.	Can identify, through experience or complex data analysis, where exceptions need to be made to the original process and that these are managed effectively to maximise the opportunity. Looks beyond price to drive added value through supplier collaboration - even to writing shared category strategies where applicable. Looks beyond the category management approach to understand the extra benefits that can be delivered. Researches similar markets and products/services to identify other approaches and trends that are relevant in a benchmarking capacity and how that could be applied to improve the sourcing approach. Knows when to change KPIs or SLAs to provide increased focus in key performance areas.

MC2 Production systems

Example profile

	1 - Understands	2 - Executes	3 - Transforms
Knowledge	Has a basic understanding of different production systems available and examples of their application e.g. Total Productive Maintenance (TPM), effective housekeeping, Single Minute Exchange of Die (SMED), good manufacturing practice. Understands the principles of the Plan-Do-Check-Act cycle. Understand OEE measurement and can describe constituent parts. Is aware of the basic operational costings that underpin decisions made and prioritisation of actions (including total maintenance cost).	Has a detailed knowledge of different production systems, and has experience of applying them (including SMED, effective housekeeping such as 5S, and good manufacturing practice). Understands the philosophy and key elements of the chosen maintenance approach and why it is a good fit to existing operations (product type, customer, legislation). Understands asset and product costings to a sufficient detail to be able to make balanced decisions from an asset perspective. Is fully aware of the standard operating parameters and trigger points for actions. Understands the use of charters in defining meeting objectives, inputs, outputs, involvement and decision rights. Can demonstrate how visual reporting can highlight performance versus target and help communicate key priorities. Understands the qualification process for new products, equipment and materials. Can identify and eliminate external changeover elements.	Has experience of production systems and their implementation in a number of situations (ideally in different organisations and/or industries). Can clearly define the relative benefits of each and their 'fit' with the current operation. Has experience of different overall maintenance strategies (e.g. run to failure, asset duplication, spares pooling) and the relative benefits of each depending upon product/customer/market factors. Has a detailed knowledge of any relevant ISO accreditation requirements. Has sufficient knowledge of production systems and manufacturing methodologies to carry out training of these across the organisation.

Application	Can interpret an OEE result by correct analysis of the constituent parts, and is aware of the key triggers that drive OEE. Has sufficient knowledge of chosen systems and KPIs to identify current performance. Is aware of the basic daily/weekly meeting structure employed within the operations area and the purpose of each meeting type. Has used meeting charters in establishing effective review meetings, and has been involved in developing/updating charters.	Makes objective decisions on actions by balancing operational performance and cost (linked to budget controls). Uses knowledge of the chosen manufacturing methodology principles (e.g. TPM) and total cost of maintenance in shaping daily approach including meeting structure and agendas, performance reviews, planning of activity/actions and prioritisation. This includes rotational focus on items such as safety, quality, and cost. Can set and communicate required standards within the operation and design regular audits to monitor compliance. Can break KPIs into in-process measures and identify how supporting processes should support the measures. Can design processes to drive consistency of approach whoever takes on a job (such as job card clarity, intervention planning, visual standards). Can accurately interpret process review mechanisms (automated such as condition monitoring or manual such as performance meetings) to ensure that planned downtime is optimised.	Able to define required knowledge management as part of an overall qualification process including training, updated process control and maintenance. Has defined factory level scorecards and reporting templates. Experienced in leading large change initiatives within manufacturing and can use loss analysis to define and prioritise improvement roadmaps. Sets the overall maintenance strategy (generally as a result of previous experience in other organisations) for the current operation that are best matched to the process, having the right balance of corrective and preventative maintenance to minimise the total cost of maintenance. Can lead Blitz Kaizen type approaches to rapid operational improvements. Uses knowledge of previous applications to establish tolerance levels for new process/ equipment. Experienced in eliminating external elements and streamlining of internal elements within changeover reduction plans.

MC2 Production systems

Example profile

	1 - Understands	2 - Executes	3 - Transforms
		Has used Short Interval Control charts within the operation to track real-time performance and prioritise actions. Can apply rapid changeover methodology to define all individual elements as external or internal. Can calculate OEE, including implementing from scratch where necessary.	Can develop qualification protocol with clearly defined success criteria for safety, quality, efficiency and costs. Can used structured assessments to monitor standards and identify outages for improvement.
Control	Is aware of known root causes for common issues and so can quickly apply judgement in resolving exceptions/failures. For known focus areas can monitor trended performance and identify when action is required (including experience of using Pareto analysis to assess and prioritise issues). Applies sound knowledge of cost/benefit equations in determining best fix for issues and issue prioritisation. Uses knowledge of area and standard operating parameters to challenge when things change.	Uses judgement in determining when to act outside standard processes in resolving issues (such as accelerating a planned maintenance or component replacement activity, bringing forward a plant stop). Uses recognised tools to target improvements in the performance of own operation/area (e.g. changeover reduction, fault proofing, condition monitoring). Can Identify where an issue is not a one-off (including applying statistical process control principles) and proposes actions to resolve including increased maintenance frequencies, or change to more proactive techniques.	Interprets trend analysis on root causes to identify routes to preventing recurrence through redesign of processes and/or equipment - including work with providers on technology solutions. Can use mean time between failures and touches measurement to support productivity improvement. Has extensive experience of setting improvement agendas. Brings specialist skills in areas of design (fault proofing such as Poke Yoke), changeover time reduction, intervention planning and optimisation, to improvement groups and major incident follow-ups, ensuring all options considered in developing targeted actions.

	Can Identify where an issue is not a one-off (including applying statistical process control principles) and proposes actions to resolve including increased maintenance frequencies, or change to more proactive techniques. Can lead reliability reviews with appropriate analysis (e.g. Pareto, root cause) to determine prioritised actions (with equal focus on soft and hard causes). Can set realistic targets for OEE and agreed KPIs based upon performance data and specific improvement areas. Can define team and individual metrics that they can influence and contribute to department and site KPIs. Knowledge of Failure Mode Effect Analysis (FMEA) in analysing process risk. Is able to accurately interpret condition based monitoring outputs to ensure timely decisions.	Can coach/train team members in a wide range of performance improvement techniques. Has sufficient industry knowledge to benchmark existing performance (including failure rates, OEE) and identify action areas. Has the ability to 'engineer out' key process failures where existing approaches have been unsuccessful. Is able to translate changes to overall maintenance strategy into updated processes. Can identify areas where further data analysis (through better use of system tools, or specific analysis software) will drive increased understanding.

DC4 Contractor management

Example profile

	1 - Understands	2 - Executes	3 - Transforms
Knowledge	Aware of which logistics elements have been outsourced, and who the key contractors are in this sector. Has a clear understanding of what services 3rd parties offer, and the benefits they could bring in terms of scale, expertise, channels to market etc. Can describe the key risks of engaging a 3rd party, and quantify these (in terms of impact and cost). Understands how to monitor KPIs and act accordingly with any contractors involved.	Understands cost base of existing transport network and drivers of cost. Can apply knowledge of cost base to effectively compare responses from potential contractors. Understands value and risks that a 3rd party could bring to an operation. Fully aware of costs and benefits of using 3rd parties and how performance is best managed. Understanding of 3rd parties costs/ economics, and the value that they should bring.	Clear view of cost base, benefits/risks of 3rd party involvement. Good understanding and explanation of how best to engage with 3rd party providers in developing a positive on-going relationship.
Application	Is aware of the process for managing and reviewing the performance of a third party, from contract terms to Service Level Agreements (SLAs). Can manage data from multiple sources (internal & 3rd party) to aggregate up meaningful metrics to manage contractor performance. Able to generate 'like for like' comparisons between different 3rd-party operators.	Can identify gaps/restrictions in existing logistics network, where 3rd party support may be beneficial. Is able to effectively engage with potential 3rd party partners and describe win/win opportunities. Able to articulate service differentials in contractor responses and can turn this into a review of value add to the organisation, allowing for the effective choice of the most suitable partner.	Has experience of working with a 3rd party as they develop a 'new' service that adds value/competitive advantage and is not currently available. Works closely and proactively with the Procurement function in developing new 3rd party networks.

Control	Ability to understand the 'root causes' of why the responses from different potential contractors differ, and assess how each would affect the company. Is aware of the historic performance for outsourced services (i.e. whether they have improved since moving to 3rd party) and is able to support decision making on next steps/appropriate future targets.	Able to shape how best 'outliers' in responses/performance from contractor should be analysed. Sets meaningful/stretching targets based on what 3rd party can/should be able to deliver. Able to engage with 3rd parties so that they are pro-actively coming up with potential improvements.	Understanding of what a 3rd party should be able to bring to an organisation, and how to focus 3rd parties on delivering greatest value. Able to engage with 3rd parties so that they are pro-actively coming up with potential improvements. Aware of operators in tangential markets, what they offer and what might be sensible to translate into own market. Understands alternative contract models, including pricing, service and incentives and is able to evaluate their fit with business requirements.

SC1: Demand forecasting management

Example profile

	1 - Understands	2 - Executes	3 - Transforms
Knowledge	Understands the forecasting business process and techniques used. Able to explain and articulate implications of poor forecast accuracy and bias on the business. Understands why products are grouped for forecasting and how each family is treated. Can explain the basic demand step and how forecasts are incorporated into the Planning process. Understands the different components of the forecast (e.g. time series, event based) and has a clear view of their relevance to the business. Understands the difference between a plan and a forecast.	Can influence decision making through an understanding of the implications of forecasts on business plans and performance. Able to reorganise forecasting product groups, based on their sales/marketing characteristics, and decide which forecasting techniques are applied to each group (e.g. top down, bottom up, causal, seasonality, exponential). Is clear on other factors that will influence demand for chosen products (e.g. weather, seasonality linked to holidays, changing trends). Tracks forecast progress and identifies significant gaps versus actuals, diagnoses causes and potential solutions. Challenges commercial plans based on evidence in order to establish the best view of the future.	Identifies opportunities for process change where forecast accuracy, stability or bias is poor. Has a good understanding/experience of best proven practice forecasting methods and can implement new techniques where they will add value. Can optimise product families to drive overall end-to-end supply chain benefits such as inventory reduction or lead time improvement (supply chain integration). Develops supplier relationships to support promotions as 'business as usual' and configures the supply network to cope with promotional activity. Sets appropriate criteria for promotion performance so that everyone is clear when off track. Influences commercial team to ensure that there is supply capacity in place to fulfil promotions.

Application	Can compare forecasts to plans and identify/understand implications from that, and have relevant conversations with stakeholders (e.g. customers, marketing, account managers). Can identify unexpected/unrealistic demand forecasts from previous knowledge/experience or awareness of different agendas, and is able to constructively raise concerns in the right forum. Understands that forecasts have risks and uncertainty, and is able to communicate the level of risk appropriately.	Is clear on which forecasting technique to use for producing the best forecasts (e.g. statistical, causal, exponential). Can generate forecasts at the required level of detail to drive business planning processes. Can explain the rationale and assumptions used to generate the forecasts and gain buy in. Is able to translate issues seen in day to day approach back to the forecasting process and implement improvement based on lessons learned. Conducts scenario planning within existing boundaries to help shape opinion and forecast accuracy (including promotional effects and new products). Ensures input data to forecasting process is complete and validated. Ensures data collection process is effective.	Uses knowledge of customers and wider Sales and Operations Planning cycle to identify opportunities to align/improve system and process timings to ensure the most accurate forecast data. Influences the forecasting process through improved engagement and alignment with senior managers within Sales and Marketing functions. Is involved in budget setting/review process challenging targets based upon in-depth knowledge of historic and future market conditions. Has identified data requirements outside existing systems and sourced these to improve accuracy. Identifies and implements ways to integrate strategic suppliers, including information and risk sharing. Understands how changes in promotional activity may influence supply chain requirements, and works with other internal functions to ensure strategies for this are developed.
Control	Is able to identify where forecast data is outside of expected tolerances, and escalate as necessary. Can analyse forecast accuracy using defined guidelines/parameters and resolves/ escalates as appropriate.	Able to identify gaps in existing knowledge that limit the forecast accuracy, and build a plan to rectify (such as improved market intelligence, product trials). Effective review of demand plan assumptions based upon actual sales, identification of potential automation opportunities to improve speed of analysis and allow more time to focus on decision review, understand levers (and historic effectiveness) to meet any budget gaps.	Uses knowledge of systems and scenario planning to develop improved ability to automate parameters, remove duplicated data and identification of faults/mistakes at source (both within internal systems and in data sharing with customers). Has set an improvement agenda that is clearly aligned to overall business strategy. Automate the process to allow more time for review and option generation - identifying where value is added in the process and allocating most time to this.

Foundation

FC1 Integrated supply chain

Example profile

	1 - Understands	2 - Executes	3 - Transforms
Knowledge	Has knowledge of best practice across the supply chain and thought leadership as applicable to the organisation. Has an understanding of the end-to-end supply chain, and can therefore describe the key interactions, the key strengths and weaknesses, and the main stakeholders within it. Has an understanding of the company structure, and the roles and responsibilities of each department. Is clear on the main cross functional processes (such as Sales & Operations Planning , New Product Introduction etc.) and the cycles for these. Can describe the basic scope/purpose of each functional unit, and how it links to adjacent functions. Can describe the key functional trade-offs that exist in delivering the overall organisational objectives.	Strives to understand the end-to-end supply chain and the broader business environment. Has a view of key trends which will affect the business and the supply chain over the next few years. Has an understanding of the end-to-end supply chain, the key interactions, for the organisation and industry, and an understanding of the roles of suppliers, partners and customers. Is aware of the supply chain type that the organisation is operating to (e.g. lean, agile, replenishment), and can describe the key attributes associated with that. Can define how the supply chain strategy has been applied to the approach within their own role/department.	Is a thought leader in cross-supply chain and integrated supply chain practices, and constantly challenges the status quo to drive sustainable improvements. Understands the most common types of supply chain (e.g. lean, agile, replenishment) and is clear on how to define a supply chain strategy to suit each of these examples. Can describe the typical functional trade-offs that accompany different supply chain strategies, and identify which is most suited to the current configuration and why. Understands best practice for the industry in which they operate.

Application	Has knowledge of the main business processes, cycles, calendars, objectives, inputs and outputs of each stage. Understands the main communication channels within the company, and how each is used. Has knowledge and understanding of the standard metrics in use, why they are measured, and what 'good' looks like. Communicates and describes the objectives and inputs and outputs of the key supply chain processes and planning cycles. Liaises with key supply chain stakeholders to align common supply chain objectives.	Drives standards throughout the business in metrics and business processes. Uses standard metrics and business processes in day to day working, based on an understanding of what they mean and the behaviours they drive. Uses communication channels effectively to drive cross-functional understanding and optimisation. Uses formal business processes and cycles effectively to manage the business. Follows company standards. Can describe how each function's objectives relate to the overall organisational objectives. Ensures that there is standardisation of metrics between functions to support a transparent review of performance in achieving organisational goals - not those in functional silos.	Sets standards based on knowledge of internal and external supply chain and cross-industry best practice and can pinpoint which element(s) of the process is (are) lacking where there is a large gap between current and target levels. Ensures that internal communications are fit for purpose, and drives improvement where required. Pro-actively drives programmes to ensure cross-functional supply chain knowledge across the organisation. Ensures that the organisation structure, metrics and company processes support integration and effective communication. Has previously reviewed the supply chain 'needs' within an organisation and shaped and implemented a supply chain strategy to best meet these needs. Defines an integrated supply chain strategy that fits with company objectives and customer needs.
Control	Understands acceptable limits for the chosen supply chain metrics, and the remedial actions required if outside these limits. Can explain the impact/effect of not following standards in relation to adjacent functions. Monitors the acceptable limits for the chosen supply chain metrics, and suggests the remedial actions when outside these limits.	Actively monitors potential risks within the existing supply chain processes, such as the known 'weak links'. Is able to review/reflect on actual events/ performance and can demonstrate that they have fed this into the process of improved thought leadership. Drives to eliminate functional silos and ensures that there is standardisation of metrics between functions to allow for most transparent review of performance in achieving organisational goals.	Drives reviews of company business processes, metrics and standards to improve end to end performance and effectiveness. Is a strong advocate of metrics and process standards. Is able to spot talent and opportunities across functional boundaries and encourages a break from traditional approaches to exploit these (e.g. increased mobility across functions, change of ownership of parts of the operation to Plan or Deliver teams).

15 The assessment process and outputs

As outlined in the introduction, this process is designed to create action to develop the necessary people capabilities to deliver business plans.

There are four key stages in the process of applying capability insight to specific roles and development plans. The approach can be tailored to each organisation but the standard elements are as follows:

1. Define the scope
The framework has been designed to be both modular and customisable. By selecting specific profiles from the full tree shown in Figure 1. the scope can be defined. For these chosen profiles the content is then customised to reflect specific industry and organisation terminology and metrics.

The other factor that will influence the scope for any assessment is the existing organisational structure. Typically, these structures change over time, so it is not feasible to consider the capabilities required at a role level without first understanding the current organisational structure and reporting lines.

2. Identify the target capabilities
Having defined the scope for a capability assessment (the desired outcome, a tailored list of profiles, clarity on the organisational structure), the next step is to define the level of capabilities needed to achieve this, by individual role.

Ideally this would be done in conjunction with the sc**prime**® process profiles, although this is not essential.

Taking each of the chosen roles in turn, the selected capability profiles are defined against the three levels:

Understands: aware of scope, measurement and impact
Executes: effective day-to-day delivery and control
Transforms: able to drive step change improvements and establish new work methods

The resulting scoring defines each role in terms of the capabilities required to deliver the desired outcomes.

3. Assess the existing capabilities

Having identified the target capabilities, the next key step is to assess existing individuals against the required standards. This stage uses the same profiles, but requires a strong knowledge of the current abilities within the chosen teams.

There are a number of available options for completing an assessment of existing capabilities, linked to the size of the team and the culture within the business.

The most effective way of completing this process is by self-assessment but with the results being moderated and challenged by departmental heads. However, if more appropriate, rapid assessments can be carried out directly by the line managers for each of the roles reporting to them.

The precise score is determined by considering an individual's skills against each of the statements within the chosen capability profiles. This should be carried out at a detailed level, as the intention of this scoring is to identify specific gaps, not just general areas.

4. Clarify the action plans and training

Creating a summary of gaps at a role level can quickly show if there is a specific area of weakness shared across a number of roles. However, the real aim of this process is to identify specific needs by person/role and, therefore, to prioritise any training, development or recruitment to help close gaps.

The detail is drawn out by analysing the missing capabilities across all of the roles and prioritising actions based on a combination of potential risk and cost/benefit.

In agreeing the required actions, there is a range of different delivery methods that should be considered, with the focus being on delivering targeted, value adding actions. Typically, this will be a combination of the following approaches:

- **Changing role scope/organisational structure:** there may be cases where the required capabilities exist within other members of the team. In some cases, a change in roles or a change in role scope may be the fastest way to obtain the capabilities needed

- **Group training modules:** in situations where a skills gap is identified across several team members, a focused training event involving simulations or technical 'How To' guides is ideal

- **Individual training options:** where individual gaps are identified, the solution could involve specific training events plus elements of work shadowing, participation in other business projects and self-development

The worked example in the next section demonstrates how the process can be applied to a typical scenario, and the outputs that are generated throughout the four main stages.

16 Uses of the framework

Some organisations have integrated the sc**prime**® people capability framework into their Human Resources processes, with each role in the organisation defined by a set of required capabilities.

The sc**prime**® people capability framework can support a variety of business needs:

- It can be used to identify the target capabilities needed to deliver the strategy (or implement improvement programmes) and determine any gaps that currently exist
- It can be used to drive consistency of skills across a number of global regions and improve role profiles
- It can be used as part of an annual assessment process to determine individual development needs and training requirements

It can also be used to:

- Identify the right people for the right jobs
- Ensure there is a sustainable balance of skills across teams/functions
- Benchmark skill levels against industry standards and/or internal improvement metrics
- Tightly specify the capabilities and skillsets required in new recruits

The aim of using the framework is to identify actions to support delivery, and the process for this is summarised in the diagram below.

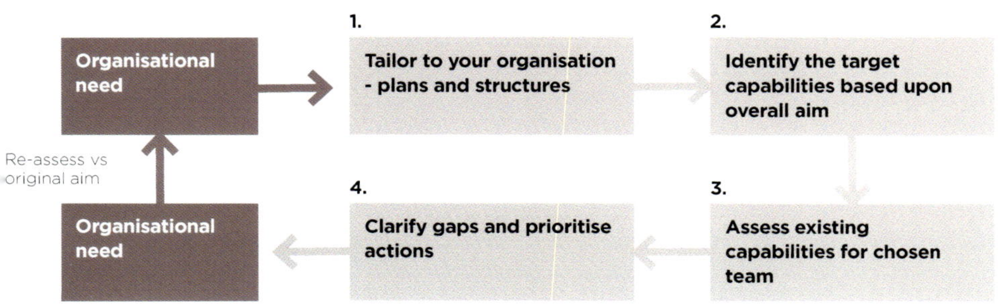

Example scenario: Defining the capabilities needed for a team

Background

A recently appointed Supply Chain Director wants to improve the effectiveness of the planning team. The team consists of both long-standing staff and newer recruits, each having a different type of role profile and a variety of opinions on the scope of roles within the department. To improve the cohesion of the team and its subsequent delivery using existing processes, the Supply Chain Director decides to use the people capability framework as an objective assessment improvement process.

Approach

1) Define the scope

The focus of this work surrounds four key members of the planning team and their ability to deliver a range of existing processes. The roles are:

- Supply Chain Manager
- Demand Planner
- Supply Planner
- Materials Manager

The start point is to identify the capability profiles that are relevant to deliver the individual roles effectively. This is done by selecting from the overall list of available profiles.

The Supply Chain Director does this based on a clear idea of how the department will be operating in the future. Using the Supply Planner role as an example, of the 29 capability profiles available within the framework 11 are selected as being key to succeeding in the role. The example on the next page shows an extract of these, with a brief explanation of their relevance.

Plan **Role profile: Supply Planner**

Role scope The Supply Planner role is the integration point between the production and demand planning functions within an organisation. Their ultimate goal is to manage the delivery of the forward plan agreed by the business through the S&OP cycle. Working with the Demand Planner to understand future demand expectations and priorities, the Supply Planner will plan supplies from the business' production facilities and work to ensure continuity of supply. The Supply Planner will plan around the constraints of operational capacity.

Key accountabilities

- Develop supply plans to fulfill the agreed demand plan
- Review production capacities and highlight concerns to relevant production staff
- Interact with production to understand future capacity constraints and take actions to mitigate
- Identity and escalate as appropriate any potential supply issues
- Work may involve the use of capacity planning software and tools
- Handle demand exceptions, working with production and demand planning to resolve
- Develop inventory strategies on existing items, new products, and product phase-outs
- Works very closely with demand planning & production

Functional area	Capabilities profiles	Relevant?	Capability summary
Plan	S&OP	Yes	• Co-ordinates the monthly supply cycle • Maintains key supply cycle KPIs & can identify root causes of trends
	Finished goods inventory management	Yes	• Understands the links and trade-offs between inventory and service • Understands how to use inventory to sensibly mitigate supply issues
	Supply management	Yes	• Understands and can make use of the capacity planning tool • Fully understands the supply network and its key constraints
	New product introduction	Yes	• Understands the NPI forecasting process • Works with production to develop ramp up plans to support NPI
Buy	Sourcing and category management		
	Supplier management and development	Yes	• Understands the NPI forecasting process • Works with production to develop ramp up plans to support NPI
	Operational purchasing		
	Materials management and planning	Yes	• Understands the NPI forecasting process • Works with production to develop ramp up plans to support NPI

Note that to deliver their role effectively, there are as many capability requirements in other functions as there are within the 'home' function of Plan.

2) Identify the target capabilities

The team then considers each role in turn, to identify the required level of capability across all of the selected profiles.

Using the Supply Planner example again, the output of this process for the 11 chosen profiles may look as shown on the next page.

Supply Planner: target capabilities

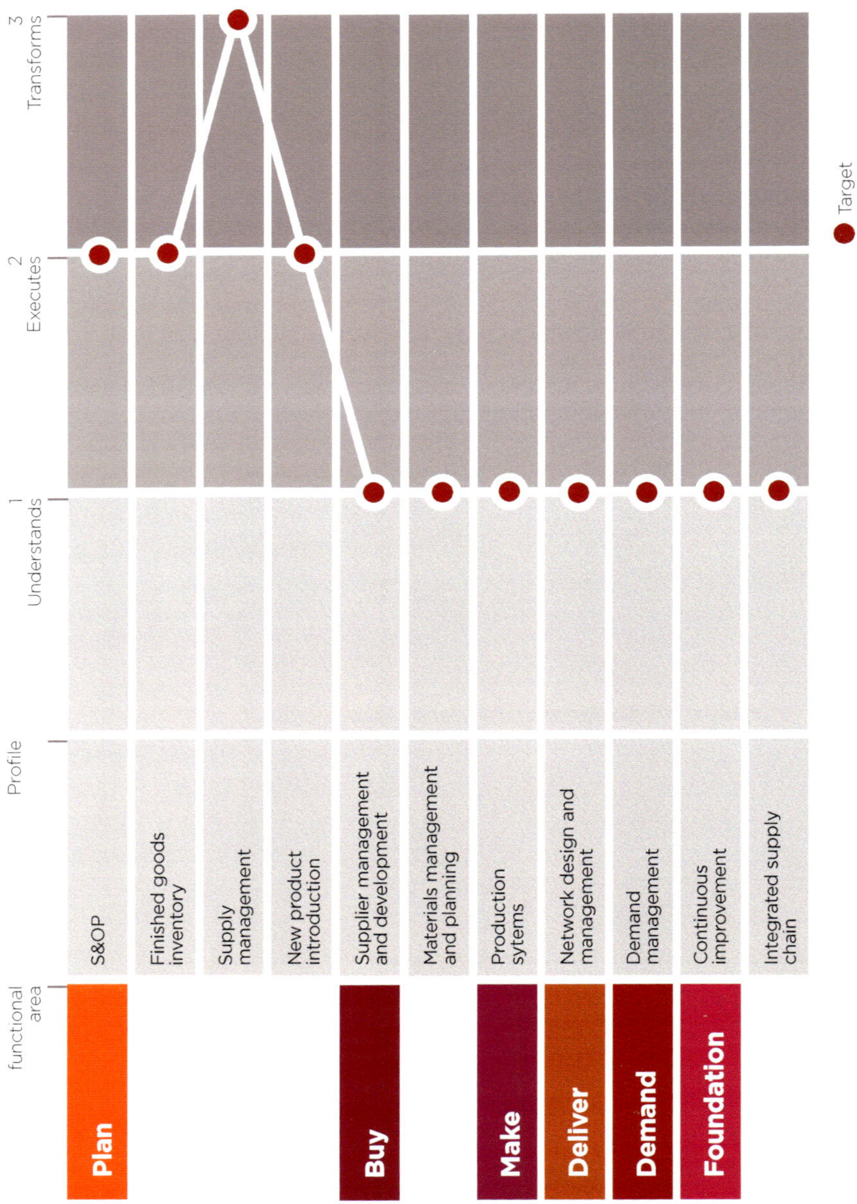

3) Assess the existing capabilities

For a relatively small team size, as with this example, the role holders themselves are asked to self-assess against the chosen capability areas. This approach ensures a high level of buy-in to any resulting plans.

The role holders are aware that target scores have been created, but are not shown these targets in advance.

The project team then meets with each person in turn to review the self-assessment, discussing this further and agreeing a final assessment score based on demonstrated evidence of previous delivery.

The final scores are then calculated by considering how many of the defined capabilities are demonstrated by each role holder. Where an individual possesses all of the capabilities to reach level 1 (Understands), but only 2 of the required 10 elements of level 2 (Executes), this is scored as 1+(2/10) or 1.2. For each individual, a snapshot of capabilities can therefore be created, as in the example for the Supply Planner on the next page.

Supply Planner: target and actual capabilities

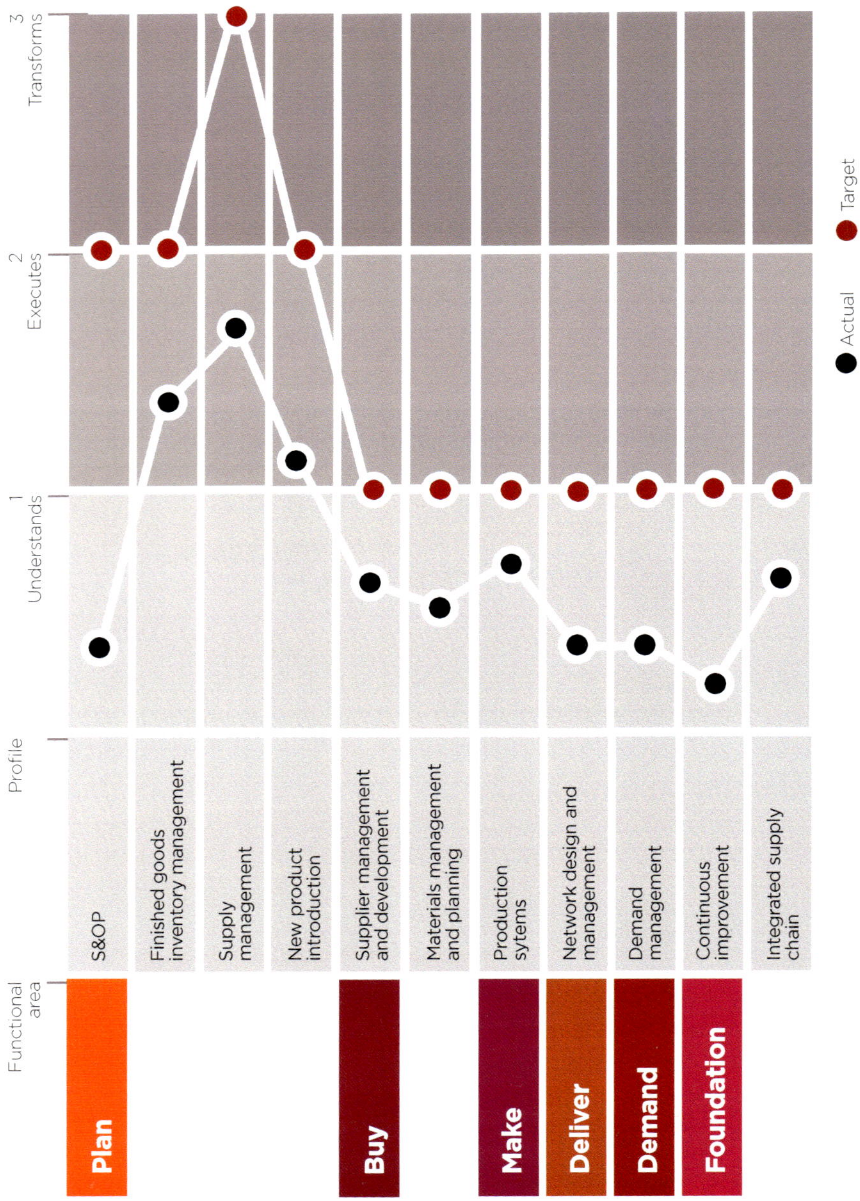

4) Clarify the action plans and training

Having identified where capability gaps are present, the next key step is to clarify what those gaps are and prioritise suitable actions to resolve them.

In the example of the Supply Planner, the gaps are not only within the Plan processes but also in a lack of understanding of how these processes fit within the wider supply chain approach. The solution for this individual would therefore focus on a mixture of training on the concepts that underpin that approach and allocating time to spend with adjacent functions to improve awareness. This is captured in a development plan, and an example extract from one of these is shown below.

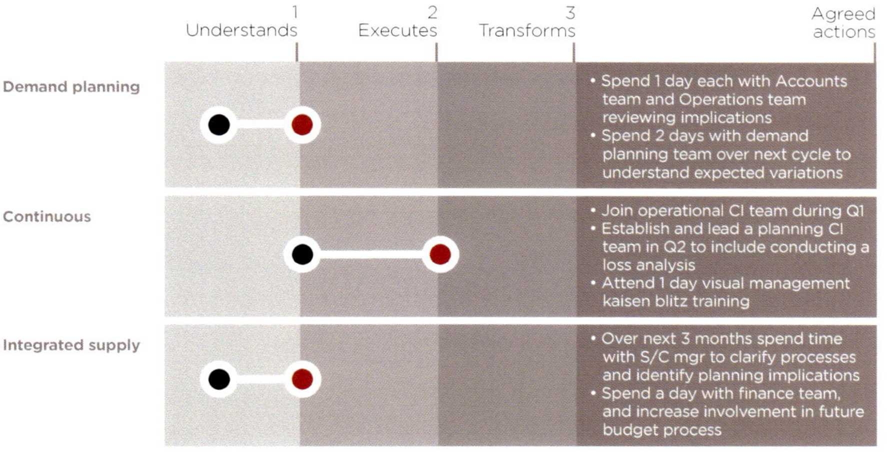

Summary:

The people capability framework allows development to be focused where it is most needed. A more traditional approach by the Supply Chain Director at the outset could well have meant that the start point for this 'new' team was to focus inwardly on the planning processes. Using the framework shows that the greatest benefit will actually be derived from getting the team to look outward, focusing on their part in making wider supply chain processes more effective.

17 Frequently Asked Questions (FAQs)

What is the scprime® people capability framework designed to do?
However good a business plan is, it requires skilled and capable people in order to be successful. This framework helps businesses ensure that their teams are an enabler of that success rather than being seen as a blocker of change.

What are the specific benefits of using the scprime® people capability framework?
The benefits of using this framework result from improved delivery of business plans – either improved quality or improved pace. This happens as potential people capability issues are highlighted in advance, and therefore can be addressed proactively.

What are the outputs of the process?
This process results in a set of development actions that are focused on the delivery of agreed business plans. By linking these development actions to specific processes and individuals, they are highly tailored to each business. Outputs will include a range of training solutions that are designed to add value rather than just improve general knowledge and understanding.

Where do the profiles come from?
The profiles are based on delivering and working with best practice supply chain processes and the people responsible for them. This experience is drawn from hands-on roles in 'blue chip' organisations across many industries, combined with over a hundred consulting engagements focused on delivering the most effective actions. They describe the capabilities needed to deliver the sc**prime**® process capabilities. As such, they go beyond describing generic skills; they pinpoint the technical skills and experience that are needed to be effective in delivering improved supply chain performance.

Are the profiles suitable for all teams/organisations?
Any organisation can benefit from being able to better describe the technical skills their teams need, and from being able to create far more specific development plans as a result to close any gaps. The modular framework can be easily tailored to reflect different needs or structures, allowing assessment across a wide range of industries and organisations. Whatever the application,

this framework allows an objective review of capabilities across a business and results in focused actions aimed at maximising potential.

What if all profiles are relevant to a role; will it become unmanageable?
Arriving at the required scope for a role is a key part of the assessment programme. It is important that assessors do not include the 'nice-to-haves' as a safe option. The capability levels are deliberately intended to help distinguish between those directly responsible for a process and those that need a full understanding but are not directly involved. Many people may have a wider knowledge than that, based on previous roles and experience, but if this is not directly part of their current role then it should be omitted for this process. This ensures that the gaps that are ultimately identified are directly linked to delivering the desired process plans, and that identified actions are as value-adding as possible.

The majority of roles can be described as a combination of own functional profiles, adjacent functional profiles and some foundation capabilities, with a total number of profiles ranging from 5 to 12.

How much time will it take, and what type of resource will be required?
A typical assessment takes 6-8 weeks to complete, covering tailoring to the organisation, establishing target levels and assessing existing capabilities. The resulting actions would then be prioritised and delivered.

Establishing target levels requires the input of local 'subject matter experts' in appropriate functions to ensure alignment with business processes. The assessment phase requires input from local managers, with potential HR support. The key to this is an objective, accurate assessment in order to create buy-in to the process.